WHAT IS A PRIEST?

IS VOLUME

53

OF THE

Twentieth Century Encyclopedia of Catholicism

UNDER SECTION

V

THE LIFE OF FAITH

IT IS ALSO THE

21ST

VOLUME IN ORDER OF PUBLICATION

Edited by HENRI DANIEL-ROPS of the Académie Française

WHAT IS A PRIEST?

By *JOSEPH LÉCUYER, C.S.Sp.*

Translated from the French by LANCELOT C. SHEPPARD

HAWTHORN BOOKS · PUBLISHERS · *New York*

253
L w

First Edition, July, 1959

CONTENTS

CHAPTER I

THE PRIESTHOOD OF THE APOSTLES

One day the Apostle Paul had occasion to make certain observations to the Christians of Corinth on the behaviour to be observed during what he called "the Lord's Supper" which commemorated the Last Supper of Jesus before his passion; he reminded them of the official teaching on the subject: "The tradition which I received from the Lord, and handed on to you, is that the Lord Jesus, on the night when he was being betrayed, took bread, and gave thanks, and broke it, and said, Take, eat; this is my body, given up for you. Do this for a commemoration of me. And so with the cup, when supper was ended, This cup, he said, is the new testament, in my blood. Do this, whenever you drink it, for a commemoration of me" (1 Cor. 11. 23–5).

These details, thus circumstantially recalled, must have been fresh in the memories of all; it was still very close, at the most fifteen years (more or less), to the events related and Paul is at pains to remind them that this is the traditional teaching, coming from our Lord, the teaching of the whole Church.

A NEW SACRIFICE

There can be no doubt that in St Paul's mind (and in the minds of those to whom his letter was addressed) we are here concerned with a genuine sacrifice, the Eucharist, instituted by Christ; he speaks of the new covenant in his blood because he is thinking of another sacrifice which of old sealed the covenant contracted on Sinaï: Moses, after reading to the people the Book of the Covenant, took the blood of the sacrificial victims and sprinkled it on his hearers saying, "Here is the blood of the covenant which the Lord makes with you" (Exod. 24. 8). Thus Jesus showed himself here in his rôle as Mediator of the New Testament and also in his high office of Priest, offering his sacrifice, the sacrifice of his Body and Blood in which was sealed the new and eternal covenant with the new people of God.

In choosing bread and wine as the signs of his sacrifice he also had in mind, of course, that other mysterious priest whom Abraham encountered after his victory: "And as he came back, the King of Sodom went out to meet him at the valley of Savé, which is the same as the Royal Valley; Melchisedech, too, was there, the king of Salem. And he, priest as he was of the most high God, brought out bread and wine with him" (Gen. 14. 17–19). This episode, which might seem unimportant at first sight, did not remain in oblivion, and Psalm 109 proclaimed that the future Messias would not only be king but "priest for ever in the line of Melchisedech". Following the Epistle to the Hebrews, Christian tradition adopted this teaching and St Cyprian compares the bread and wine of the Supper with the Canaanite priest's offering which the canon of the Roman Mass continues to commemorate as a prophetic image of the eucharistic sacrifice.

Thus Christ at the Supper instituted a new sacrifice; so well did St Paul understand this that previously in the same letter to the Corinthians he contrasted our Lord's chalice and our Lord's table with the chalice and table of evil spirits, that is, with the sacrifice offered to idols (1 Cor. 10. 21). In consequence the Christians of Corinth possessed a sacrifice which perpetuated that of the Supper and so obeyed our Saviour's command, "Do this for a commemoration of me".

"DO THIS FOR A COMMEMORATION OF ME"

These last words implied something else besides for there is no sacrifice without its priest. If then, as St Paul says, in the Eucharist Christians ought to herald the Lord's death until he come (1 Cor. 11. 26), and if we are here concerned with a sacrifice and a sacrificial meal, it is absolutely necessary that there should be a visible priesthood lasting until the end of time.

The apostles received the order to do what Christ did at the Supper; the first Christians understood very well that this did not mean merely a material repetition, but in real truth a sacrifice with which they must be united, must share in all together, as the apostles did with Christ. At this table of the Lord there will always be, therefore, a priest to preside, to bless, to give thanks and to represent the Master and repeat his actions. As the Anglican theologian Dom Gregory Dix has truly said, "he who broke the bread and pronounced the thanksgiving had in himself all the powers of a priest".

Just as at the Last Supper all ate and drank, but one only, Christ himself, performed the function of a priest, so was it to be afterwards and until the end of time: all Christians take part in the Eucharist, all in a certain sense bless and break the bread, for all the community unites in the liturgical rite and communicates in the unity of the one same Lord: "We have a cup that *we* bless; is not this cup *we* bless a participation in Christ's blood? Is not the bread *we* break a participation in Christ's body? The one bread makes us one body though we are many in number; the same bread is shared by all" (1 Cor. 10. 16–17). But these words of St Paul do not exclude the special office of a priest who presides in the place of Christ, as the most ancient liturgies bear witness and as the whole trend of our Lord's command requires: "Do this in memory of me." This order given to the apostles constituted them priests of the new sacrifice and, according to the words of Session 22 of the Council of Trent, commanded "them and their successors in the priesthood to offer the Body and Blood of Christ. . . . So has the Catholic Church ever understood and taught."

ANOTHER CHRIST

Thus in the eucharistic liturgy the apostles and their successors hold the place which Christ held at the Supper. The priest who gives thanks and consecrates does not do so in his own name nor even as the representative of the community; he represents the Christ of the Supper, he repeats his actions, he is his image, his visible and living sign.

The Fathers of the Church insist upon this necessity of reproducing as closely as possible what happened at the Supper. "He alone", writes St Cyprian in his sixty-third letter, "fulfils the office of priest in the place of Christ who does what Christ did, nor does he offer to God the Father in the Church the truth and fullness of sacrifice except in so far as he offers as he sees that Christ himself offered." And the anonymous Roman commentator of the end of the fourth century, known as Ambrosiaster, commenting on the first Epistle to Timothy, asserts that the priests of the Church are the substitutes, the vicars of Christ.

But we must go even further. Not only is the priest who celebrates the image or, according to the expression of Hesychius of Jerusalem, the figure of our Saviour, but our Saviour is present in him in a certain manner, he clothes him, so to say, with himself: "Those who have been chosen in Christ and established in the priesthood have for their magnificent priestly and holy vestment Christ himself." This metaphor of Cyril of Alexandria's, explaining the prophecy of Malachias, may be amplified by other no less telling images. Eusebius of Caesarea, preaching at the consecration of the Church of Tyre, declares that Christ dwells in his ministers and continues to offer through them. Gregory Nazianzen, in the course of an admirable sermon on baptism, compares the priest to a ring bearing the seal of Christ: whether the ring is of gold or iron the impression made in the wax is the same; thus whatever the personal holiness of the priest the effect produced is the same, for it is the same Christ acting through him. At the beginning of the sixth century, a remarkable letter of Severus of Antioch summarizes this teaching:

The priest who stands before the altar, while he plays a purely ministerial part, pronounces his words as holding the place of Christ and reproduces the rite which was accomplished when Christ instituted the sacrifice for his apostles; he says over the bread, "This is *my* body which is delivered for you, do this in memory of *me*"; and in the same way over the chalice he says the words "This chalice is the new Covenant in *my* blood, which is shed for you". Consequently it is Christ who even now makes the offering and it is the power of his divine words which effects the expected result so that the bread and wine become his Body and Blood.

Such is the teaching of tradition which the Council of

Trent summarizes in the famous phrase comparing the Mass not only to the supper but to the cross: "There is one and the same victim, one same offerer who offers himself through the ministry of priests and who then offered himself on the cross; it is only the manner of offering that is different."

There can hardly be cause for surprise, then, at the appearance of another expression whose precise origin is doubtful but which can now be encountered in the official documents of Pius XI and Pius XII—the priest is another Christ, *alter Christus*.

"RECEIVE THE HOLY SPIRIT"

The events of the Last Supper were completed during a mysterious scene whose details have been preserved for us by St John; it was the evening of Easter day and the apostles were gathered together:

> And now it was evening on the same day, the first day of the week; for fear of the Jews, the disciples had locked the doors of the room in which they had assembled; and Jesus came, and stood there in their midst; Peace be upon you, he said. And with that, he shewed them his hands and his side. Thus the disciples saw the Lord, and were glad. Once more Jesus said to them, Peace be upon you; I came upon an errand from my Father, and now I am sending you out in my turn. With that, he breathed on them, and said to them, Receive the Holy Spirit; when you forgive men's sins, they are forgiven, when you hold them bound, they are held bound. (John 20. 19–23.)

Together with the power of consecrating and distributing the Eucharist the apostles were also to have the power of forgiving sins. Now there can be no doubt whatever that this is a sacerdotal power and the Council of Trent in its twenty-third session mentions it in close connection with the power of offering the Eucharist as a prerogative of the ministerial priesthood: "If anyone says that in the New Testament there is not a visible and external priesthood or that there exists no power of consecrating and offering the real Body and Blood of Christ and of forgiving and retaining sins, let him be anathema."

So well did St Thomas understand this close union of the two powers that he considered them as being essentially a single power, and so he asserts in his commentary on Distinction 18 of the fourth book of the Sentences of Peter Lombard: "Since every grace and every remission of sins in the mystical Body is derived from the Head of that Body it seems clear that it is essentially the same power which endows the priest with authority to consecrate the Eucharist and to bind and to loose sins . . . it is merely a difference of concepts according to whether this power is considered in connection with its different effects."

The scene related by St John, therefore, has clear priestly implications and the Fathers often understood it as a real ordination. Particular emphasis must be laid on the meaning of Jesus' action in breathing upon his apostles and saying to them "Receive the Holy Ghost". For the Christian priesthood has always been considered as an anointing by the Holy Spirit, a sharing in the anointing received in his humanity by him who, according to the meaning of the Hebrew *Messias* and the Greek *Christos*, is the anointed One in the highest sense of the word. This anointing by the Holy Ghost, effected invisibly in Jesus when "the power of the most High" overshadowed Mary and visibly after his baptism by John the Baptist, is continued in the apostles. "Spirit", in Semitic languages as well as in Greek and Latin, means also *wind*, the *breath of life*. Here again St Thomas clearly explains the meaning of this anointing in his commentary on John 20: "The Holy Ghost came down first on the apostles as a breath to indicate the spreading abroad of grace effected in the sacraments of which the apostles were the ministers; that is why Christ said, When you forgive men's sins, they are forgiven."

The Greek word used by the evangelist to describe Jesus breathing on the apostles is the same which in Genesis describes God breathing into the nostrils of the man he had just formed from the clay of the ground; the same word is used again in Ezechiel's vision (Ezech. 37. 9) foretelling the resurgence of Israel as a new people of God. It signifies a communication of divine life, of that life of which the risen Christ merited the power of pouring forth on men and which he infused into his apostles and priests for them to become in their turn its beneficiaries and ministers. Like every ordination of a priest the scene in John 20 includes an interior transformation of the apostles, a spiritual gift which makes them sharers in the lifegiving strength of the risen Lord.

THE PRIESTLY CHARACTER

This gift of the Spirit to the apostles did not transform them principally for their own sakes, for their personal holiness, but rather for the sake of others that they might remit or retain sins and do what Christ did at the Last Supper in memory of him, that is, reproduce among men his sacrifice and remit sins by virtue of this same sacrifice. It is a grace which is more for the benefit of others than for the recipient himself.

There took place in the apostles, as there was to take place in their successors, a profound though invisible transformation analogous, according to St Gregory of Nyssa, to that which occurs in the matter of the sacraments. He deals with this subject in a sermon on the baptism of Christ:

> The bread is at first ordinary bread but when it has been offered in sacrifice it is called and is in reality the Body of

Christ. . . . It is the same efficacy of the Word which also makes the priest exalted and venerable, since by his additional blessing he becomes different from the ordinary people. For only yesterday he was just an individual among the rest of the people and lo! he has suddenly become a leader, a president, a master of worship, a teacher of hidden mysteries. This takes place without any bodily or external change in his appearance, but his invisible soul, by an invisible power and grace, has been transformed into a higher state.

On the other hand, since, as has been pointed out, the personal holiness of the priest is not in question, and even grave sins do not impair his priestly power, it must be concluded that the priesthood of the apostles and their successors effects in them an indelible reality, a *character* analogous to that produced by baptism and confirmation. A Christian priest is a priest for ever and is never re-ordained.

It was in the struggle against Donatism particularly that the Church was obliged to state clearly traditional teaching on this point. This heresy came into being at the beginning of the fourth century in Africa; Cæcilian, the Archbishop of Carthage, had been consecrated by Felix of Aptonga, a *traditor* during the Diocletian persecution, that is, he had delivered up the Scriptures to the pagans. The partisans of Donatus contested the validity of this consecration as if the consecrator by reason of his sin had lost his priestly power. Already condemned by the Council of Rome in 313, and by that of Arles in 314, they were opposed particularly by St Optatus of Milevis (*c.* 366) and by St Augustine. Against the Donatists these two great bishops defended the traditional teaching that, like the anointings of baptism and confirmation, that of the priesthood is not effaced by sin, and loss of sanctifying power does not entail the disappearance of the priestly character.

"In the same way", writes St Augustine in his book *Of Baptism against the Donatists*, "that whoever has received baptism does not lose it by withdrawing from unity, so he who has received the sacrament of Orders does not lose it if he cuts himself off from unity" (Bk. 1, ch. 1).

This teaching of the Catholic Church would be found astonishing only by one who did not understand that the apostles and their successors in the priesthood are not priests of themselves, that they are only the representatives, the vicars, of the one High Priest, who acts in and through them, independently of their holiness and personal merits.

THE GIFT OF THE SPIRIT AT PENTECOST

The apostles, therefore, were already priests before Christ's Ascension. But in order to accomplish the whole of their mission in the world they were to receive a new outpouring of the Holy Spirit on the day of Pentecost, a new *strength* (Luke 24. 49; Acts 1. 8) to make them fit to be Christ's witnesses "in Jerusalem and throughout Judaea, in Samaria, yes, and to the ends of the earth".

This word *witnesses* seems to explain fully the purpose of this new gift of the Spirit granted to the Twelve. They are conscious of being witnesses on very special grounds which distinguish them from the rest of believers, even though the latter received the Holy Ghost. This consciousness of constituting an organized body entrusted with the special mission of bearing witness is clearly shown in St Peter's speech in the first meeting of believers gathered together to await the coming of the Spirit: the Twelve were not alone, for one hundred and twenty persons were assembled who "gave themselves up to prayer, together with Mary the mother of Jesus, and the rest of the women and his brethren" (Acts 1. 14). But Peter stood up and recalling the betrayal by Judas declared, "There are men

who have walked in our company all through the time
when the Lord Jesus came and went among us. . . . One
of these ought to be added to our number as a witness of
his resurrection". Matthias, who was elected, "took rank"
with the eleven apostles (Acts 1. 15–25).

To be a witness in this special sense befitting the Twelve
it is not, therefore, sufficient to have lived with Jesus, to
have been present during his life and at his teaching: they
are witnesses "appointed beforehand" (Acts 10. 41), chosen
from among all, members of a special body of which Peter
is the head. And on the day of Pentecost the Holy Spirit
was given to them in such a way that they alone could
communicate him by the rite of the imposition of hands
(Acts 8. 14–17).

It is therefore certain that the apostles received at Pentecost an additional grace qualifying them more immediately
and more definitively for their mission which was to be
continued by the bishops. Should the descent of the Spirit
in the form of tongues of fire be seen therefore as the
equivalent of a real ordination to the priesthood or to the
episcopate? Many writers have thought so and oriental
theology in particular continues to teach it. In the west,
on the other hand, the theology of the sacrament of Orders
has not paid much attention to Pentecost and this has often
resulted in insufficient account being taken of the part of
the Holy Ghost in the Christian priesthood. As it is not
our purpose to dwell on controversies of detail it must
suffice that we have called attention to passages in the
Acts which, as a result of the coming of the Holy Spirit,
attribute to the Twelve a special strength to enable them
to be the official witnesses of the resurrection. And in fact
it is only subsequently that we see the beginning of the
public preaching of the Gospel and the foundation and
organization of the Churches. The title "witnesses of
Christ" expresses their privilege so clearly that it is always

reserved by the Acts (with the one exception of the case of the martyr Stephen, Acts 22. 20) for the members of the apostolic college; and when St Paul, incorporated in this body, wishes to characterize his own mission he uses this term (Acts 22. 15; 26. 16). If, then, as we shall see, the bishops are the successors of the apostles, in them in some sense will be found the continuation of the grace of Pentecost, making them witnesses of the risen Christ.

CHAPTER II

THE BISHOPS, SUCCESSORS
TO THE APOSTLES

In the early non-canonical Christian writings the priestly function of the apostles is not often explicitly mentioned; it would be wrong to find cause of astonishment in this for many reasons which it will be sufficent merely to enumerate here: the fewness of these writings, the often secret character of Christian worship during the periods of persecution and especially the unquestioned belief of the early Christians to whom it was purposeless to recall the priestly character of the Twelve.

Eusebius, however, has preserved for us a letter from Polycrates of Ephesus to Victor I (188–99) in which the author considers the apostle St John "who rested on the Lord's breast and who was a priest" as the successor of the High Priest of the old Law, enjoying the privilege reserved to the latter of wearing a plate of pure gold hanging over the forehead (Exod. 28. 36). In the same way the apocryphal literature which begins to proliferate during the second century often gives clear evidence of the sacerdotal character of the apostles in connection with the offering of the Eucharist: according to the *Acts of John* before his death the apostle offered the holy sacrifice and gave communion to the faithful "asking for each of the brethren that they might become worthy of the grace of the Lord and of the holy Eucharist". The apostle St Andrew declares to Aegeas, the proconsul: "Daily I offer a sacrifice to the one true and almighty God, not the smoke of incense, nor the flesh of bellowing bulls or the blood of goats, but I sacrifice daily on the altar of the cross the unspotted Lamb who remains the immortal and living Lamb after all the faithful people have eaten his flesh and drunk his blood." Similar accounts will be found in the acts of the apostles Peter and Thomas. All these passages, despite their often curious nature, at least show clearly the well-established belief of the sacerdotal character of the apostles.

ST CLEMENT OF ROME'S LETTER

Before the appearance of the apocryphal Acts of the Apostles a voice was heard which proclaimed the existence of the priesthood in the Church, connecting it with the powers received by the apostles and describing it in continuity through them with the priestly institutions of the Old Testament; these passages from St Clement of Rome's *Letter to the Corinthians*, written during the last years of the first century, are too important to be omitted and extracts from the most important passages referring to our subject are here quoted from chapters 40–4:

> We are obliged to carry out in fullest detail what the Master has commanded us to do at stated times. He has ordered the sacrifices to be offered and the services to be held, and this not in a random and irregular fashion but at definite times and seasons. He has moreover himself by his sovereign will determined where and by whom he wants them to be carried out. . . . A special office is imposed upon the priests; and special ministrations fall to the Levites. The layman is bound by the rules laid down for the laity.
>
> Each of us, brethren, must in his own place endeavour to

please God with a good conscience, reverently taking care not to deviate from the established rule of service. Not everywhere, brethren, are sacrifices offered—be they perpetual offerings, or votive offerings, or sin offerings, or trespass offerings—but at Jerusalem only; and there offerings are not made in every place, but in front of the sanctuary. . . . The apostles preached to us the Gospel received from Jesus Christ, and Jesus Christ was God's ambassador. Christ, in other words, comes with a message from God, and the apostles with a message from Christ; both these orderly arrangements, therefore, originate from the will of God [The apostles preached the Gospel] and from among their earliest converts appointed men whom they had tested by the Spirit to act as bishops and deacons for the future believers. . . . What wonder, pray, if [they] appointed the above-mentioned officials, seeing that also the blessed Moses . . . when the priesthood had become an object of jealousy . . . [said to] the leaders of the twelve tribes, "Brethren, God has chosen for his priestly service that tribe the rod of which will bud. . . ." Our apostles, too, were given to understand by our Lord Jesus Christ that the office of the bishop would give rise to intrigues. For this reason, equipped as they were with perfect foreknowledge, they appointed the men mentioned before, and afterwards laid down a rule once for all to this effect: when these men die, other approved men shall succeed to their ministry. Consequently, we deem it an injustice to eject from the sacred ministry the persons who were appointed either by them, or later, with the consent of the whole Church, by other men in high repute and have ministered to the flock of Christ faultlessly, humbly, quietly and unselfishly. . . . Indeed, it will be no small sin for us if we oust men who have irreproachably and piously *offered the sacrifices proper to the episcopate.*[1]

[1] Clement of Rome, *Epistles to the Corinthians*, 40–4; Eng. trans. by James A. Kleist, S.J., in *The Epistles of St Clement of Rome and St Ignatius of Antioch*, pp. 34–6. (Ancient Christian Writers series).

Thus St Clement reminds the Corinthians, who had re-volted against their pastors, of the rights of the latter: as in the Old Testament there were not only precise liturgical laws concerning the circumstances of the different sacri-fices but also a priestly hierarchy established by God and by Moses on God's command, so in the New Testament Christ, the Father's ambassador, whom the writer calls in a later chapter "the high priest and master of our souls", in his turn sent the apostles who likewise instituted bishops and deacons: Christians therefore must respect these arrangements as the Jews were obliged to respect those of the Law concerning the priesthood and their liturgical services. The whole context of these pages makes it clear that Clement is speaking of the transmission of a priest-hood from Christ to the apostles and from them to their successors, the bishops, and also the deacons who are com-pared to the Levites of the Old Testament.

FELLOW WORKERS WITH THE APOSTLES

Both these categories (of bishops and deacons) are to be found in the New Testament and Clement of Rome's evidence can assist us to a better understanding of the inspired books concerning the successors of the apostles.

St Paul, as we have seen, concluded his account of the Last Supper and the institution of the Eucharist written to the Corinthians with the words, "So it is the Lord's death that you are heralding, whenever you eat this bread and drink this cup until he comes". If Christians by cele-brating the Eucharist are to herald the Lord's death until he comes, obviously the priesthood must endure until the end of time and, as a consequence, the apostles must have successors in the priesthood. And in fact, from the very beginning, there are to be found other persons who, in the Christian community, perform the functions more or less belonging to the priesthood. These persons are called either apostles or bishops or presbyters or deacons.

In the first place there are other apostles besides the Twelve. This title is given to Paul who lays claim to it insistently; it is also applied to Barnabas, possibly also to Silvanus and Timothy (1 Thess. 2. 7) and to others mentioned in 1 Corinthians (12. 28). The number of twelve, chosen by Jesus himself in connection with the twelve tribes of Israel, in no wise appears as a maximum: it symbolizes the continuity between the Old and New Testaments, for the propagation of the Gospel began with the twelve tribes, but other peoples of the earth were soon to be joined to the people of Israel in the same work of propagation of the new people of God.

Nevertheless, the use of this name was limited; it appears that even James of Jerusalem may not have borne it according to one reading of Galatians 1. 19.[2]

James, nevertheless, occupied a place of prime importance in Jerusalem, from the very first years of the preaching of Christianity; he appears as the leader of the local community in Jerusalem, endowed with considerable authority, especially among the Christian converts from Judaism. If he was not an apostle, as seems very likely, what title should he be given? The New Testament is not clear on the point, but in the middle of the second century we have precise evidence on the matter from Hegesippus, a Palestinian who visited Rome during the pontificate of Anicetus (155–6) and remained there until the time of Eleutherius (174–89). Hegesippus informs us in his *Memoirs*, fragments of which have been preserved by Eusebius, that "James, the Lord's brother, received [the administration of] the Church with [or, after] the apostles":

[2] Instead of "I did not see any of the other apostles except James, the Lord's brother" (Knox) some translators (e.g. Fr Lyonnet in the French *Bible de Jérusalem*) have "I saw no other apostle [than Peter] but only James, the Lord's brother".

the same source, the second book of Eusebius' *Ecclesiastical History*, adds several details from which it is clear that Hegesippus regarded James as the successor of the High Priest of Jerusalem; in addition, another fragment, also preserved by Eusebius in the fourth book of his *History*, informs us that James bore the title of Bishop of Jerusalem and that Simeon succeeded him in that office. James, therefore, was a bishop, and it seems clear that to Hegesippus he was as such a sort of Christian successor to the Jewish High Priest. Without inferring from this all that certain recent writers have endeavoured to do and without exaggerating the position of James in the Church, as still more recently O. Cullmann seems to do in his work on St Peter, it is certain nevertheless that historically James was regarded by the Christians as possessing a real priesthood during the actual lifetime of the apostles, and as exercising at Jerusalem with considerable authority, according to the clear evidence of the Acts and the Epistles of St Paul, the functions of a bishop.

THE FIRST BISHOPS

This title of bishop (*episcopos*) is to be found in several places in the canonical writings of the New Testament. Already before Pentecost, St Peter in his discourse concerning the filling of the place of Judas, used the word *episcope* to designate the apostolic office left empty by the traitor (Acts 1. 20). This word had already been used in the Greek translation of the Bible (known as the Septuagint) to denote the office entrusted to Eleazar, Aaron's son: "under his care . . . all that concerns the worship paid in the tabernacle, and all the furniture of the sanctuary" (Num. 4. 16). The word *episcopos* had not so precise a meaning in Jewish usage prior to Christianity as it was afterwards to enjoy; applied to men it designated civil magistrates, military leaders, overseers or inspectors of a building under construction, as well as priests or Levites whose functions concerned public worship.

The Acts of the Apostles and the writings of St Paul inform us that certain persons of the primitive Church, invested with very wide powers, bore in their turn the title of bishop (*episcopos*). It was certainly a title of honour, for St Peter does not hesitate to use it to designate Christ himself, the supreme Head of his Church (1 Peter 2. 25) and St Paul solemnly asserts: "It is well said, When a man aspires to a bishopric, it is no mean employment that he covets" (1 Tim. 3. 1).

Some of their functions are clearly indicated: as presidents of the communities, with powers as judges and heads, they are responsible for the faithful entrusted to them as shepherds are for their flocks. Although their liturgical and priestly functions are not mentioned in so many words it seems difficult not to discern allusions to them in a number of passages in the pastoral Epistles and in the Acts of the Apostles: the bishops are set over the Church of God (1 Tim. 3. 5), over a community in which liturgical prayer occupies an important place (1 Tim. 2) and in which, we may be sure, the Eucharist was celebrated in accordance with our Lord's command. This link between the episcopate and the priestly offering of the Eucharist, although not explicitly mentioned in the New Testament, is however clearly vouched for in the earliest non-canonical Christian writings; in addition to Clement of Rome's *Epistle to the Corinthians*, quoted above, we have on this point the evidence of the *Didache* (chs. 14 and 15) and especially that of St Ignatius of Antioch: "Let no one do anything touching the Church, apart from the bishop. Let that celebration of the Eucharist be considered valid which is held under the bishop or anyone to whom he has committed it."[3]

[3] Ignatius of Antioch, *Letter to the Smyrnaeans*, 8, in Kleist, *op. cit.*, p. 93.

This passage from the *Letter to the Smyrnaeans* shows that at the time of St Ignatius, during the first decades of the second century, others besides the bishop could, under his authority and delegation, carry out the office of a priest and even offer the Eucharist; we are obliged to think of those bearing the name of presbyter who, in the letters of Ignatius, are clearly distinguished from the bishops. But it is not certain that this distinction between the two terms bishop and presbyter existed from the beginning and in the New Testament it may well be that they were synonymous and designated the same persons. We may note at this point—though the problem is further explored below —that the term presbyter when it designates an official function in the Church is always used in the plural in the New Testament (save in 2 and 3 John in which the author uses the term of himself); on the other hand, the term bishop is almost always in the singular (save in Acts 20. 28 and Phil. 1. 1). It is possible that both were used indifferently on occasion to designate in general all the authorities in charge of a Church without stating precisely whether the episcopal or presbyteral power was intended in the present use of the terms. But very rapidly, as we shall see, a clear distinction grew up between the lesser priests and the bishops, the latter being in a special manner the successors of the apostles.

THE LAYING-ON OF HANDS

This idea of a continuity, a succession between the apostles and those whom they put in charge in the Church, an idea whose clear expression we encountered in Clement of Rome, appears in the New Testament connected with the external rite of the laying-on of hands.

In 1 Timothy Paul tells him: "A special grace (*charism*) has been entrusted to thee; prophecy awarded it, and the imposition of the presbyters' hands went with it; do not let it suffer from neglect" (1 Tim. 4. 14). And in the very first lines of 2 Timothy Paul repeats, "I would remind thee to fan the flame of that special grace (*charism*) which God kindled in thee when my hands were laid upon thee" (2 Tim. 1. 6).

Thus twice the Apostle mentioned the laying-on of hands received by Timothy and the similarity between the two passages is too striking for it to be thought that they refer to two different occasions; this laying-on of hands was performed by a *presbyterium*, a body of presbyters, but of this body Paul himself formed part and was sufficiently important in it for him, in the second passage quoted, to disregard the others and mention only his personal action.

By this external rite of the imposition of hands Timothy received a special grace which remained in him permanently. Moreover, this special grace is conferred for a proper performance of the task entrusted to the Apostle's youthful disciple; the context makes it clear that it is a question of a *spirit*, "a spirit of action, of love, and of discipline," which Paul himself received from God and which now is communicated to Timothy: "The spirit he has bestowed on us is not one that shrinks from danger" (2 Tim. 1. 7). There is a continuity, therefore, between the spiritual grace received by the Apostle and that which he has communicated to his disciple by the laying-on of hands.

In his turn Timothy possesses the power of the imposition of hands for the making of presbyters (1 Tim. 5. 22); it is the same with Titus in Crete and the passage concerning the latter (Titus 1. 5) shows clearly that these presbyters were also bishops, or at least that the bishop is one of them.

This collection of texts establishes the fact of a genuine succession, of a continuity between the *charism*, the special grace, received by St Paul and that which, received by Timothy and Titus, is transmitted by the imposition of hands to those whom the latter appoint as bishops or presbyters; this has always been the teaching of the Catholic Church, and it is that also of many non-Catholic theologians, notably in recent years A. Ehrhardt. We are here confronted with the first manifestation of the sacrament of Orders, an external rite conferring a grace for the exercise of an official ministry in the Church.

The rite of the laying-on of hands can be illustrated by a well-known scene from the Old Testament in which Moses transmitted his powers to his successor Josue: "So Moses did as the Lord had bidden him, presenting Josue before the high priest Eleazar and the whole assembly, and there laying his hands on Josue's head, and repeating all the charge which the Lord had given him" (Num. 27. 23). This quotation is further explained by the final verses of Deuteronomy: "Josue the son of Nun, full of the gift of wisdom since Moses laid hands on him" (Deut. 34. 9). Moses' action was not merely one designating his successor to the people: it is described as efficacious, as conferring a special gift, the spirit of wisdom communicated to his successor for him to continue his task of leading the people of God. And it was the same with the laying-on of hands which makes bishops and priests.

We do not know if it was Christ himself who instituted this rite; neither at the Last Supper nor on Easter evening do we find him laying hands on his apostles; but in any case there can be no doubt that it was by his command and on his instructions that the apostles did so and passed on the practice to their successors. In fact, this is the rite that is to be found constantly throughout liturgical history for the ceremony of consecration of bishops.

THE FIRST RITUAL OF EPISCOPAL
CONSECRATION

Evidence that the laying-on of hands is indeed the traditional rite for the consecration of bishops and the communication of the priesthood of the apostles to their successors
is to be found in the important work of Hippolytus of
Rome, *Traditio Apostolica*, which was written about 215.
According to this valuable little book, when a bishop is
consecrated the consecrating bishops lay their hands upon
him; then one of them recites an admirable prayer giving
utterance to the effects of the sacramental rite. After recalling that God in the Old Testament instituted leaders
and priests and made provision for the liturgical worship
of the sanctuary in Jerusalem, the consecrator asks for
similar graces for the bishop-elect: "And now send forth
this strength which comes from you, this power of the
sovereign spirit that you have given to your well-beloved
Son Jesus Christ, and that he has given to the holy apostles
who built your Church in the place of your sanctuary (in
Jerusalem) for the glory and unceasing praise of your
name."

In the new sanctuary, which is the Church, the bishop is
made a sharer in the grace of the Holy Spirit which Christ
received in his humanity and which he communicated to
the apostles: as a leader and a priest he shares in the kingly
power and sovereign priesthood of Jesus communicated to
the Twelve and their successors.

With the words used by St Peter in the prayer before
the election of Matthias in the place of Judas the consecrating bishop continues the invocation:

Lord, *who knowest the hearts* [cf. Acts 1. 24], grant to
your servant whom you have chosen for the episcopate that
he may feed your holy flock and blamelessly exercise your
sovereign priesthood, by serving you night and day; may

he make your countenance favourable and offer you the gifts of your holy Church; may he have the power of remitting sins by the power of the Spirit of the sovereign priesthood, according to your command; may he confer orders on the clergy according to your directions and may he loose every bond by the power that you have given to the apostles.

So the bishops are clearly "the successors of the apostles, sharing in the same grace of the sovereign priesthood and the magisterium", as Hippolytus says again in the first pages of his *Elenchos*. The value of the evidence of this Roman author is the greater since it is the first link in an uninterrupted chain of similar testimony in all the Christian liturgies: Hippolytus' prayer of episcopal consecration is to be found substantially in almost all the sacramentaries of later centuries. Moreover, even in those which do not agree with it literally, the priestly and apostolic character of the episcopate is shown with impressive unanimity; the bishops, as successors of the apostles, are successors in their priesthood of which they enjoy the fullness. Thus, to quote only this example, the consecratory preface of the Roman Pontifical concludes with these words which Pius XII declared (November 30th, 1947) to be the sacramental form of episcopal consecration: *Comple in sacerdote tuo ministerii tui summam* ("Perfect in your priest the fullness of your ministry"); these words are introduced by an admirable exposition of the priesthood of Aaron, a prophetic type of the Christian priesthood. The laying-on of hands by the consecrating bishop continues to effect in our twentieth century what Paul effected by laying his hands on his disciple Timothy.

THE FULLNESS OF THE PRIESTHOOD

Very rapidly, moreover, the distinction between two degrees of priesthood, that is, between bishops and presbyters, came to be shown in the clearest fashion; it is already manifest at the beginning of the second century in the Churches to which St Ignatius of Antioch wrote. This superiority, as priests, of the bishops over the presbyters is expressed in many ways: for long the word *sacerdos* (priest) signified purely and simply only the bishop, while for the presbyter was added the significant qualification *sacerdos secundi ordinis* (priest of the second rank).

Other formulas were no less expressive: Tertullian names the bishop *summus sacerdos* (high priest); the Council of Sardica, in 343, in its tenth canon speaks of "the highest degree . . . in the divine priesthood"; Pseudo-Dionysius places the bishop at the highest point of a priestly hierarchy which he compares to the hierarchy of the heavenly spirits; and it is the established practice everywhere in the west to attribute and reserve to the bishop the *fullness* of the priesthood.

Even more characteristic, if possible, is the fact, emphasized by the studies of Mgr Andrieu on the liturgical documents of the Middle Ages, that on several occasions episcopal consecration was conferred on candidates who were not yet priests, but merely deacons, readers or even laymen; the practice appeared so normal in the eighth and ninth centuries that it is officially provided for by a Roman Ordo of the eighth century which, during the consecration of a bishop, includes the following short dialogue between the consecrator and the candidate:

"What is your status?"

"I am a deacon" [or a priest, or any other degree].

It must be admitted that episcopal consecration, at least when it is conferred on a candidate who is not yet a priest, is a sacramental rite and confers the grace of the priesthood; if it were otherwise, in that case, if the candidate were already a priest, the implication would be that it was a mere ceremony without any real sacramental efficacy.

Otherwise it would be a case of a real rite of *reordination* and it is well known that the Church has always been opposed to such a practice. It must therefore be admitted that the episcopate is always a sacrament, that it is the sacrament of Order in its highest degree of fullness.

WESTERN CONTROVERSIES

Yet whereas in the east the sacramental nature of the episcopate was never seriously doubted, in the west the same does not hold true after the end of the fourth century. In actual fact, the apostolic authority of the bishops was not questioned; they have always been considered as the apostles' successors and the word *episcopatus* is frequently treated as a synonym of *apostolatus*. But some people came to hold that at the sacramental level there was no difference between the priest and the bishop, the distinction of the two degrees of the hierarchy being based only on a difference of jurisdiction. The occasion giving rise to this theory was a purely disciplinary question; during the pontificate of St Damasus the deacons in Rome had acquired a position of such importance that they regarded themselves as superior to ordinary priests. Against such a claim an anonymous Roman author (known as Ambrosiaster) and particularly St Jerome protested vigorously; but their arguments are not always devoid of error. In order to defend the superiority of priests over deacons they could find no better means than the pure and simple identification of the priesthood with the episcopate so far as its sacramental nature is concerned. Jerome even considers, basing his conclusions on the writings of the apostles, that in the primitive Church there was no distinct episcopate and that it was a body of presbyters who, collectively and without a responsible head, governed the local Churches.

St Jerome's opinion gained ground and for many centuries influenced western theology without ever achieving definitive recognition; even at those periods when the most famous theologians considered the episcopate as only a dignity or a higher jurisdiction the traditional teaching was always defended by a certain number of theologians and especially by canonists.

The Council of Trent was unwilling to define whether the superiority of bishops over priests in relation to their orders was or was not of divine institution. Nevertheless, the Fathers solemnly declared—and that in the twenty-third session which was on the sacrament of Orders—that bishops not only belong in a special degree to the hierarchy of orders but that, on this level, they are superior to ordinary priests. Thus, since the Council, it can be said that the sacramental nature of the episcopate as an order superior to the priesthood has become almost common teaching among theologians, although the explanations of it offer certain differences. The Code of Canon Law (can. 108) goes further than the Council of Trent by stating that "in virtue of divine institution the sacred hierarchy, from the point of view of Orders, comprises bishops, priests and ministers" while other degrees have only been added by the institution of the Church.

THE GRACE OF THE EPISCOPATE

But the Council of Trent also recalled the fact that if Orders are a sacrament they are therefore an outward sign conferring a grace. Consequently, it can be asked what is the particular grace received by the bishops, the successors of the apostles, at their special consecration. It cannot be different from that charism mentioned by St Paul to Timothy which fitted him properly to carry out his task. But by attention to the data of tradition it is possible to reach an even clearer idea of the grace of the episcopate.

On several occasions St Irenaeus describes it as a *definite charism of truth,* similar to that received by the apostles on the day of Pentecost. Irenaeus' characteristic expression has been repeated in our own times by the anti-modernist oath prescribed by Pius X which is still required nowadays on a great number of occasions: "I maintain with the greatest firmness and I shall maintain until my last breath the faith of the Fathers on the subject of a definite charism of truth which is, has been and always will be in the episcopate as successors of the apostles." This charism establishes the doctrinal authority of the apostolic body and makes it a body of authentic witnesses whose infallibility is guaranteed. In this respect the grace of episcopal consecration concerns the episcopal body's power of *magisterium.*

St Irenaeus also considers the bishops as the heads "to whom the apostles have entrusted the Church", and Hippolytus of Rome, too, in the prayer of consecration quoted above, prays that the bishops may have a charism which will make them capable of being the leaders and high priests of the people of God. Indeed, this aspect of the grace of the episcopate is connected with the first-named for in each it is a question of guiding the people by the apostolic *word.* Severianus of Gabala in a homily on Pentecost, of which fragments have been preserved in the exegetical *Catenae* on the Acts of the Apostles, gives striking expression to this implication of episcopal consecration:

> Why did the apostles receive the tongues of fire on their heads? Because they were ordained as teachers of the whole world; now ordination is never performed save on the head. The coming down of tongues on the head is therefore the sign of an ordination. In fact, it is on the head that ordination takes place, as the custom has been maintained even to our own days. For, since the coming down of the Holy

Spirit is invisible, on the head of him who is to be ordained high priest is laid the book of the Gospel; and in this book thus laid must be seen naught else save a tongue of fire; a tongue because of the preaching of the Gospel, and a tongue of fire because it is said, "It is fire that I have come to spread over the earth".

By alluding to the rite, at that time only just introduced into the east, of the imposition of the Gospel on the head of the candidate, Severianus gives felicitous expression to the idea, frequently to be encountered in eastern authors, that episcopal consecration confers a grace equivalent to that received by the apostles on the day of Pentecost; the bishops also receive a grace of *light* and of *strength* to be witnesses, bearers of the apostolic word and the unerring guides of the people of God.

In the west, after the fifth century, and for the reasons mentioned above, the teaching of the theologians is less precise, less rich than that of the orientals. Yet even during the period when the majority held doubts about the sacramental nature of the episcopate, many popular accounts show the belief of the faithful in the value of the laying-on of hands on the new bishop. Gregory of Tours relates that the bishop Nicetius of Trier during his episcopal consecration smelt a perfume and felt a weight which rested on his head and he understood, the writer tells us, "that this weight was the dignity of his priesthood". Likewise, Archanaldus, a deacon of Angers, writing (*c*. 905) the life of St Martin of Angers relates that the saint whenever he laid his hands on a candidate saw a dove alighting on the new bishop's head.

THE TEACHING OF ST THOMAS

At the outset St Thomas, in his teaching on the sacrament of Order, found himself confronted by a somewhat complex situation: he had to explain the Book of Sentences of Peter Lombard according to which the episcopate is neither an order nor a sacrament whereas Pseudo-Dionysius, already interpreted by Albert the Great, attributes extraordinary power to the bishops and to their special ordination. From the very beginning, therefore, St Thomas felt himself able to differ from the author whom he was explaining: he allows that the episcopate is a higher order than the priesthood, in relation not to the consecration of the Eucharist but to the mystical Body. He admits that the laying-on of hands confers a grace although, in order to follow the author on whom he was commenting, he does not admit that the essence of the rite of consecration lies therein. The teaching of St Thomas became gradually more precise as he continued his commentary; without delaying over details we can summarize his principal conclusions in the following propositions:

1. The episcopate is conferred by the laying-on of hands; it is not an order in the precise sense given to the word by Peter Lombard, that is, in relation to the consecration of the Eucharist; but St Thomas speaks of *ordination*, which confers a grace, the grace of the episcopate, and also another stable and indelible effect, similar to the character conferred by the other orders. But this stable and indelible effect, which makes a bishop capable of ruling the people *in persona Christi*, is not given the name of character, once again out of loyalty to Lombard's terminology.

2. The episcopate was instituted in the first place to "govern" the people of God; the bishops are therefore primarily teachers for the essential rôle of a head, a prince, is to lead by word, to teach.

3. By their consecration the bishops receive a certain number of sacramental powers which are those precisely which concern the government of the people of God. They

are the ministers of confirmation and Orders, for these sacraments bestow a special function in the mystical Body. On the other hand, by virtue of their ordination ordinary priests do not receive these powers; if on occasion these powers are delegated to them it is always in such a way as to be capable of revocation, and St Thomas regarded them only as a power of jurisdiction occasionally granted by the bishops.[4]

4. To the latter falls also the office of distributing duties to the collaborators they have taken to themselves and to whom they entrust a portion of their pastoral ministry, just as a king delegates some of his authority to bailiffs and provosts; but the priests and deacons thus associated with the ministry of the bishop do not receive this power over the mystical Body by their ordination and on this point they remain in complete dependence on the episcopal body.

5. Concerning the consecration of the Eucharist ordinary priests possess the same power as the bishops and form with them, in this respect, one single order, the priestly order. Yet to the extent that the Eucharist produces as its fruit the unity of the mystical Body the celebrant who is a simple priest remains dependent on the episcopal body even to the point that St Thomas, while admitting the validity of the consecration, could write: "A sinful priest, deprived by ecclesiastical censure of the exercise of his orders . . . becomes incapable of offering the eucharistic sacrifice." Such a sacrifice would be valid as a sacrament but it would not be valid with regard to the fruits produced.[5]

6. Lastly, the distinction between bishops and priests is not of ecclesiastical origin; not only does it go back to apostolic times but it must be seen in connection with our Lord's own institution when he chose his seventy-two

[4] 2a, 2ae, q. 39, a. 3.
[5] 3, q. 82, a. 10 and 7.

disciples in addition to his twelve apostles. Although for some time they were known by the same name their functions were always entirely different.

Thus St Thomas finally, despite a certain hesitancy of expression owing to the terminology used by Peter Lombard, is found to hold the teaching that we have already encountered in St Irenaeus and Hippolytus of Rome: the episcopate is a separate order, an external sign conferring grace and special sacramental powers; it is the fullness of the priesthood.

CHAPTER III

THE PRIESTHOOD

At the time of Christ the members of the Sanhedrin in Jerusalem, who formed the council of the High Priests, bore the name of *presbyters*, that is, elders; the part that they played in the trial of Jesus will be remembered. Now everything goes to show that the Church of Jerusalem, as it is depicted for us in the Acts of the Apostles, was from the beginning organized on the model of the Sanhedrin with *presbyters* assisting James, the first bishop. These persons, whose number we do not know, appear to have been invested with a certain authority in dependence on the bishop; but, confining ourselves to the evidence of the Acts of the Apostles, we cannot assert that they possessed any priestly power.

The pastoral Epistles of St Paul on several occasions mention the presbyters; they are persons worthy of respect and Timothy is to be careful of their reputation; one of their functions is to preside and this requires certain qualities on their part (1 Tim. 5. 17–20; Titus 1. 6 following). There are several of them in a Church, and the word *presbyter* in the pastoral Epistles occurs always in the plural. Nevertheless they form an organized body, a *presbyterium*, with the power of laying-on hands, *together with the apostle*, to institute new ministers (1 Tim. 4. 14; cf. Acts 13. 3).

It must be admitted, however, that at the time of the

pastoral Epistles the distinction between bishop and presbyter is not clearly expressed. It is the same in St Clement of Rome's *Letter to the Corinthians*, though at one point he clarifies the question considerably: according to his teaching those who in the Christian community possess functions corresponding to those of the Old Law bear not only the name of bishops but also of presbyters:

> Indeed, it will be no small sin for us if we oust men who have irreproachably and piously offered the sacrifices proper to the episcopate. Happy the presbyters who have before now completed life's journey and taken their departure in mature age and laden with fruit! They, surely, do not have to fear that anyone will dislodge them from the place built for them. Yes, we see that you removed some, their good conduct notwithstanding, from the sacred ministry on which their faultless discharge had shed lustre.[1]

In the Letters of St Ignatius of Antioch, as has already been pointed out, the distinction between bishop and presbyter is far clearer. By them we know that in Syria and Asia Minor at the beginning of the second century the Churches were organized almost on the pattern of that of Jerusalem in the time of James, with a single bishop surrounded by a *presbyterium* forming his council. To the Smyrnaeans Ignatius writes: "You must follow the lead of the bishop, as Jesus Christ followed that of the Father; follow the presbytery as you would the apostles. . . . Let no one do anything touching the Church, apart from the bishop. Let that celebration of the Eucharist be considered valid which is held under the bishop or anyone to *whom he has committed it.*"

This final statement shows us that on occasion others besides the bishop could, under his authority and by his order, preside over the offering of the Eucharist and thus

---

[1] *Epistle to the Corinthians*, 44. Kleist, *op. cit.*, p. 36.

act as a priest; these persons could only have been the presbyters.

THE FIRST RITE OF PRIESTLY ORDINATION

This priestly character of the presbyters appears clearly in the *Traditio Apostolica* of Hippolytus of Rome, which is also the oldest explicit evidence of the ceremony of ordination to the priesthood:

> When a priest is ordained let the bishop lay his hand on his head while the other priests also touch him and let him pronounce words similar to those mentioned above, as we have said for bishops.
>
> Let him say this prayer:
>
> God and Father of our Lord Jesus Christ, look upon your servant here present and grant him the spirit of grace and counsel that he may help the priests and govern your people with a pure heart, as you looked upon the people whom you chose for yourself and commanded Moses to choose elders [i.e., presbyters] whom you filled with your Spirit that you gave to your servant. Now also, Lord, grant us to preserve ever within us the Spirit of your grace and make us worthy to serve you with faith, in the simplicity of our heart, in praising you through your child Jesus Christ, through whom are to you, Father and Son with the Holy Spirit, glory and power in the Holy Church, now and for ever and ever.

According to this prayer, the first duty of presbyters is, then, to govern the people of God in harmony with the other presbyters and in dependence on the bishop, like the seventy-two Elders to whom Moses communicated his spirit; but on the following page, in dealing with the ordination of deacons, the author states that this common spirit of the body of presbyters (priests), in which the deacons have no share, is a participation in the priesthood.

Indeed, the same work describes the sacerdotal functions of the *presbyterium*; after the consecration of the new bishop, the priests take their place around him and with him stretch out their hands over the gifts which constitute the matter of the Eucharist, while the bishop pronounces the anaphora.

To sum up, the *presbyterium* appears in the *Apostolic Tradition* of Hippolytus not as a collection of isolated individuals, but as a college or body of priests united to the bishop and forming only one with him in the guidance of the Church.

PRIESTS AND THE EUCHARIST

The sacerdotal character of the lesser priests (i.e. the presbyters) becomes increasingly clear as time goes on. Whereas Tertullian never gives them the title of *sacerdotes*, which is always reserved to bishops, St Cyprian includes them all under this term on several occasions, especially in his letters 61, 67 and 72. In his fifth letter, he also mentions, as taken for granted, that a presbyter celebrates Mass in the absence of the bishop; when the latter is present it is he who celebrates, but the priests concelebrate with him.

The multiplication of urban or rural churches gradually led the bishops permanently to attach priests to these churches, and henceforth the latter habitually offered the Eucharist in the absence of the bishop. It by no means follows that the dependent relationship of these priests to the bishop was forgotten, and this dependence was expressed on occasion by a special rite; thus at Rome the priests of the different *tituli* (the parish churches) celebrated, but the pope sent them a morsel of the bread that he had himself consecrated (called the *fermentum*) and each of them placed it in the chalice with which he was celebrating; this rite, according to the declarations of Innocent I to the Bishop of Gubbio, signified the very close union between the bishop and his priests; it was not confined to the city of Rome, or of Gubbio, but was practised in other dioceses, as we learn from the *Liber Pontificalis*.

This dependent relationship of the priest to the bishop in the celebration of the Eucharist remains in force in our own days as at the time when St Ignatius declared that there is no *valid* Eucharist save that offered by the bishop or by him to whom he had committed it; and we should recall what St Thomas lays down (quoted in the previous chapter) concerning a priest deprived by his bishop who yet continued to celebrate Mass. This dependence is made clearer still by another feature emphasized by Pseudo-Dionysius and repeated by St Thomas Aquinas: the priest only celebrates on an altar and with sacred vessels which have been previously consecrated by a bishop.

MINISTERS OF THE SACRAMENTS

In the first centuries of the Church it was only the bishop who reconciled penitents, but here, too, increasingly the episcopal body was obliged to obtain the help of its collaborators in the sacerdotal order, that is, of the priests. It must be emphasized that the extension of this power to the presbyters left them in complete dependence on the bishop; the power of absolution is given to the priest together with that of consecrating by his ordination; but he still requires *matter* on which to exercise this power just as for consecrating the Eucharist he needs bread. Now this matter, apt for absolution, that is, a Christian under his jurisdiction, is given to the priest by the bishop who has his own power as a head over the mystical Body.

The same reasoning holds good for the Last Anointing: here again the matter of the sacrament, which is the oil of the sick, is consecrated by the bishop. All the more, then, must be emphasized the dependent position of the priest for the administration of the sacraments of confirmation and Orders. By ordination alone the priest possesses no power in these two spheres, only the bishop is their ordinary minister and St Thomas gives the reason in a few words: "By Orders and confirmation the faithful of Christ are deputed for certain special offices which belong to the governing office: thus the conferring of these sacraments belongs to the bishop alone who is as the prince in the Church."[2]

If therefore an ordinary priest receives the power of confirming or ordaining it is never by virtue of his ordination but it is by a revocable and occasional concession on the part of the episcopal body; now according to the Thomistic terminology referred to above, a power that is not conferred by consecration but by a mere injunction of a superior is never the power of Orders but one of jurisdiction.[3]

Thus in the administration of the sacraments, as for the offering of the Eucharist, the simple priest appears, according to the term of the Roman Pontifical, as a *cooperator*, a collaborator, of the episcopal order who assists the bishop and continues his action while remaining in immediate dependence on him.

The same Roman Pontifical finds an expressive image in the help that the sons of Aaron were to give their father in the offering of sacrifices and in other matters of worship which the High Priest could not perform by himself; for that purpose they were made participators in the fullness of their father's priestly anointing: "To Eleazar, Ithamar, the sons of Aaron, you imparted a share of the fullness of their father's priesthood so that the order of priests might be sufficient in numbers for salutary sacrifices and for the more frequent celebration of the sacred rites."

[2] 3, q. 65, a. 3, ad 2um.
[3] 2a, 2ae, q. 39, a. 3.

This comparison between Aaron and his sons on the one hand and the bishop and his priests on the other is entirely traditional to the extent that St Jerome, who is generally silent on the distinction between bishop and presbyter, mentions it himself on several occasions, particularly in the celebrated Letter 146 to Evangelus, alluded to above.

FELLOW WORKERS OF OUR ORDER

This cooperation with the work of the episcopate is to be found in spheres besides the administration of the sacraments. The bishop is the head of the people of God, and as such it is his duty to teach the people and officially to give testimony of the faith. Here again, it appears that in the first Christian generations this was a charge reserved exclusively to the bishop: in Africa, even at the time of St Augustine, it was regarded as an unfortunate innovation for an ordinary priest to be made to preach in the presence of his bishop.

Nevertheless, as secondary churches were entrusted to the care of priests, it became the ordinary practice, at least in the absence of the bishop, for these pastors to be charged with the teaching of their flock and its entire guidance. This supreme authority, of which they thus became custodians, is theirs by participation in that of their bishop, and St Thomas compares it with the authority of bailiffs or provosts in relation to the king.

In this connection the Roman Pontifical contains valuable teaching; priests, it asserts, bear the same relation to the bishop as did the seventy elders who assisted Moses; the latter, relates the book of Numbers, complained to God that he could not bear alone the burden of the entire charge of the people on their way to the Promised Land:

Whereupon the Lord said to Moses, Choose out for me

seventy Israelites of ripe age, men already known to thee as elders and officers of the people . . . I will come down and converse with thee there; taking away some of the spirit which rests upon thee and giving it to them instead, so that they may share with thee that charge over the people which thou canst not support unaided. . . .

So Moses went back to the people, and told them what the Lord had said. Then he chose seventy of the elders of Israel, and ranged them in a half-circle at the tabernacle door. And when the Lord came down, hidden in the cloud, to converse with him, he took some of the spirit which rested upon Moses and gave it to the seventy elders instead. (Num. 11. 16–17, 24–25.)

Jewish tradition saw in this event the assertion of a fullness of *spirit*, of a *charism* of leadership, which was in Moses; the others only received it in dependence on him, without his personal power being in any way diminished, "just as", Philo remarks, "fire can light thousands of torches without being in any way impaired". Since Hippolytus of Rome, the liturgical texts describe in exactly the same terms the communication of the *pneuma*, the *spirit* of the priesthood, which is made by the bishop to the priest; the former loses no part of it, but the latter, although receiving a share in the same spirit receives it only in dependence on the bishop and his office can only be understood in this sense.

With the episode from the Old Testament must also be compared, following once more the Roman Pontifical, valuable evidence of an age-long tradition, the choice by Jesus of the seventy-two disciples (Luke 10. 1 following) who were to assist the Twelve. In all these comparisons the same idea constantly recurs; priests by their ordination do not receive a grace which enables them to feed or guide the flock of the people of God with an authority belonging to them and one which makes them real heads or leaders of the Church; the grace which they receive ordains them to be, as members of the priesthood, cooperators, fellow workers, helpers, of the episcopal body in its own function of feeding and guiding the people of God.

THE RITE CONFERRING THE PRIESTHOOD

Western theology, because it gave primary consideration to the sacramental powers conferred by Orders rather than to the grace of the sacrament, became involved in a somewhat singular controversy.

Whereas always in the east, and for ten centuries in the west, the only rite regarded as conferring the priesthood was the laying-on of hands by the bishop, in about the tenth century in the west a new ceremony was introduced which, added to the laying-on of hands, soon came to be considered as the essential rite of the sacrament. This was what was called the tradition (or "porrection") of instruments: the bishop causes each ordinand to touch a chalice containing wine and a paten with a host on it as he says for each candidate the following appropriate formula: "Receive power to offer sacrifice to God and to celebrate Masses for the living and the dead, in the name of the Lord. Amen."

It was only during the twelfth century that theologians began to consider this as the essential rite or, according to the accepted formula, the matter of the sacrament. This was not without its influence on the theology of Orders; since primary emphasis was thus placed on the powers, of which the instruments are symbols, and especially on the power to offer the Eucharist, the *charism*, the communication of the Holy Spirit of which the laying-on of hands is the sign, came to be neglected. And since none of the sacramental powers could appear higher than that of consecrating the Eucharist, the possibility of distinguishing two essential degrees of the sacrament of Order was lost to view: in fact, episcopal consecration seems to include no tradition of instruments and appears not to imply further power regarding the Eucharist; in addition, there very soon came to be forgotten what constituted the special charism of the priesthood, which is a permanent grace as *cooperator* with the bishop, and the charism of the episcopate which is a grace as *head* or *leader*; between the two there soon came to be seen only a difference of jurisdiction, and if there was still mention of the *grace* received, it was only as an increase of sanctifying grace so as to be able properly to exercise the powers conferred: there was no longer any question of a *special grace* of the sacrament for the service of the people under the dependence of the bishop.

The tradition of instruments soon came to be commonly regarded as the essential rite and the Council of Florence in 1434, setting out the common teaching of the theologians of the west, made it the subject of an official declaration in its decree for the Armenians. This is based on a small work by St Thomas Aquinas, *De fidei articulis et septem sacramentis* ("Concerning the articles of faith and the seven sacraments"). Nevertheless, this decree cannot be regarded as the infallible decision of a Council and the Church has always allowed theologians, even after the Council of Florence, to maintain that the laying-on of hands is the only essential rite and she has likewise always considered as valid those oriental ordinations which do not include the tradition of instruments.

In any case, henceforward doubt on this question is no longer possible. On November 30th, 1947, Pius XII published the constitution *Sacramentum ordinis* which laid down that the only essential rite in the ordination of bishops, priests and deacons is the laying-on of hands with the corresponding formula for each order:

In the ordination to the priesthood the matter is the first imposition of hands which is made in silence. . . . The form is constituted by the words of the preface of which the following formulas are essential and therefore required for validity: "Give, we pray thee, almighty Father, to these thy servants the dignity of priesthood; renew in their hearts the spirit of holiness, so that they may keep the office of second rank they have received from thee, O God, and gently reproach the conduct of others by the example of their holy life."

Thus a celebrated controversy has been brought to an end. It is matter for rejoicing, too, that this pontifical act enables the sacrament of Orders to be studied without the need of continual digression into useless discussion.

CHAPTER IV

THE DIACONATE

Two passages in St Paul's letters refer to the deacons in close connection with the bishops, and everything goes to show that they are thought of as occupying an important position in the churches: the Epistle to the Philippians begins as follows: "Paul and Timothy, the servants of Jesus Christ, to all the saints in Christ Jesus that are in Philippi, *with their pastors and deacons. . . .*"

And the first letter to Timothy, after enumerating the qualities of a good bishop, passes on at once to those which are expected of deacons: "Deacons, in the same way, must be men of decent behaviour, men of their word, not given to deep drinking or to money-getting. . . . These, in their turn, must first undergo probation, and only be allowed to serve as deacons if no charge is brought against them" (1 Tim. 3. 8–10).

Thus we are presented once more with an institution which goes back to the very origins of the Church; and Catholic theologians are unanimous in seeing in it a degree of the sacrament of Order: Pius XII, in the Constitution quoted at the end of the last chapter, refers to the diaconate, as well as the priesthood and the episcopate, as a part (here are the very words with which the document begins) of "the sacrament of Order instituted by Christ our Lord".

THE ELECTION OF THE SEVEN

An incident in the Acts of the Apostles is usually considered to be the account of the institution of the diaconate. The passage, at the beginning of the sixth chapter, reads:

> At this time, as the number of the disciples increased, complaints were brought against those who spoke Hebrew by those who spoke Greek; their widows, they said, were neglected in the daily administration of relief. So the twelve called together the general body of the disciples, and said, It is too much that we should have to forgo preaching God's word, and bestow our care upon tables. Come, then, brethren, you must find among you seven men who are well spoken of, full of the Holy Spirit and of wisdom, for us to put in charge of this business, while we devote ourselves to prayer, and to the ministry of preaching. This advice found favour with all the assembly; and they chose Stephen, a man who was full of faith and of the Holy Spirit, Philip, Prochorus, Nicanor, Timon, Parmenas and Nicolas, who was a proselyte from Antioch. These they presented to the apostles, *who laid their hands on them with prayer.*

This account, by itself, would certainly not be enough to prove that *deacons*, in the present meaning of the word, were chosen and ordained on that occasion, still less that these *seven* were the first deacons; reputable authorities have thought that the seven Greek-speaking deacons—it seems that they were indeed such, for they all have Greek names—were aggregated to an institution which had previously among its members only those who spoke Hebrew. Others, among them even St John Chrysostom, go further and are unwilling to allow any reference to *deacons* in the technical sense.

However, the impressive testimony of tradition on the other side must not be underrated: from the time of St Irenaeus and Tertullian, it may be called the common teaching, endorsed by the general opinion of recent theologians, including a number of Protestants. The liturgy, too, bears out this interpretation; in the Byzantine rite the example of Stephen the first deacon is invoked, and the ordination of deacon, in the Roman Pontifical, closes with this prayer: "May they be worthy to belong to the degree of those whom the apostles, moved by the Holy Spirit, chose to the number of seven, with the blessed Stephen at their head."

THE SERVICE OF TABLES

In any case the chief function of the diaconate appears to have been originally the distribution of *material benefits*. There is nothing surprising about that, if we remember that the word "diaconate" and its cognates refer primarily, in classical and in New Testament Greek, to the "service of the table". The verb *diakonein* is used to describe Peter's mother-in-law serving Christ at table (Matt. 8. 15), Martha preparing the meal while Mary listens to the Saviour (Luke 10. 40) and the master in the parable who makes his watchful servants sit and serves them at table (Luke 12. 39). However, this word *service* does refer also, by an extension of meaning, to any beneficent work, especially to works of corporal beneficence, and many examples of this wider usage can be collected from St Paul's Epistles. Eventually all service, even that of a spiritual nature, can receive this name.

But it is certain that originally in its primitive sense the word, first and foremost, was used in regard to the deacons; the diaconate was instituted in the first place as a service of *corporal mercy* for the poor, the sick and the needy in the Christian community. The Swedish theologian Riecke has shown the importance for the primitive Church of this service of beneficence, in which the deacons played the chief part. We see them at work in St Ignatius of Antioch's *Letter to the Trallians* (2. 3), and notably in *The Shepherd of Hermas*, who severely condemns "the deacons who have abused their service, who have plundered the widows and orphans, who have kept for themselves the goods which they had received for distribution" (*Similitudes*, IX. 26. 2). The *Apostolic Tradition* of Hippolytus of Rome describes them visiting the sick (c. 30), distributing to them as well as to the widows (c. 26). In the same way the Syriac *Didascalia* gives the deacon an important position: he receives the gifts of the community and hands them over to the bishop, who in his turn must distribute them to the poor; he has the duty of welcoming and looking after strangers who join the community; he is the *bishop's heart* in doing works of mercy for the poor, the sick and the needy. And the Syriac document called *The Testament of our Lord* gives clear expression to what is expected of the deacon, "the father of orphans and the poor", when it asks for him the grace of being *amatorem orphanorum, amatorem viduarum*.

St Leo the Great wrote a famous account of the martyrdom of the deacon St Lawrence "who was outstanding not only in the service of the holy mysteries, but also in the distribution of ecclesiastical goods". When the persecutor demanded of him the Church's treasures Lawrence showed him "the crowds of the faithful poor whom he had clothed and fed, thus laying up treasures which do not perish". Nothing could put in a clearer light the primary element of the deacon's mission in the Church.

THE LITURGICAL SERVICE

The organization of charitable works in the Church of the first centuries was closely bound up with the liturgical service, that is, in the first place, with the Eucharist: the "service of tables", in the sense of a service of general beneficence for the needy, was directly connected with the service of the eucharistic table, as can be seen from a careful study of the New Testament and the first Christian writers. This being so, it is to be expected that the deacon should have also a liturgical function corresponding to his status in the community.

The deacon's part in the eucharistic service, already hinted at in the *Didache* (15. 1), is vouched for by St Ignatius of Antioch in his *Letter to the Trallians* (2. 3), and described by St Justin in his first *Apology*. It is in the first place the distributing or "dispensing" of the Eucharist, and obviously links up with the deacon's function as distributor or "dispenser" of relief to the needy: when the faithful made their offerings, what was necessary for the Eucharist was gathered up and the rest put on one side to be distributed later to the clergy and the poor: the deacons were charged with dispensing both the Eucharist and the alms. Thus they offer the consecrated bread and wine to the faithful, and this right seems to have been recognized everywhere as theirs. Hippolytus of Rome, however, allows the deacon to perform this dispensation only if there are not sufficient priests.

It is also the deacon's business to "prepare the table", not only that at which the poor will be fed, but the eucharistic table itself; it is he who brings to it the *oblations*, the offerings received from the faithful. It is he again who assists the bishop or the simple priest when he celebrates the Eucharist. In this last function the relationship between the deacon and the celebrant is so close that quasi-sacerdotal expressions are sometimes used of it; the deacon St Lawrence, according to St Ambrose, reproaches his bishop for not taking with him his deacon, his minister to whom he had entrusted the "consecration" of the blood of the Saviour. In the Roman high Mass the deacon still pronounces with the priest the offertory prayer: "*We* offer you, Lord, the chalice of salvation."

But it is certain, from evidence as early as Hippolytus (c. 9) that the deacon "was not ordained to the priesthood". And when Optatus of Milevis or Leo the Great speaks of the priesthood or the priestly dignity in connection with him it has to be remembered that the sacrament of Order, of which the diaconate is part, can be called, globally, the sacrament of the priesthood.

The deacon is closely related to the priest not only in the eucharistic sacrifice but also in the administration of baptism, so that Canon 741 of the Code of Canon Law, putting the seal on a long tradition which is attested so far back as Tertullian, calls him "the extraordinary minister of solemn baptism". To these strictly liturgical functions many others were added: keeping proper order in the liturgical ceremonies, leading the prayer of the faithful: he must be respected, says St Ignatius to the Smyrnaeans, "like the law of God"; and Theodore of Mopsuestia, in his *Catecheses*, describes him as "the one who should know how to indicate the start and the finish of all that takes place in church . . . who tells everyone and reminds everyone of his proper duties and behaviour when all are united together in the Church of God".

THE HERALD OF THE GOSPEL

To the functions of the deacon already mentioned a third was added, the public reading of the Gospel. In our day this is primarily a liturgical charge, but it was originally an official commission to preach and evangelize: a deacon, Philo, seconds Ignatius of Antioch in the ministry of the word; Cyprian tells deacons to teach and to exhort the Christian people, and the *Apostolic Tradition* of Hippolytus bids them "instruct those who are present at the assembly". If we are to see in the seven in Acts 6 a group of deacons properly so called, it is clear that this function of preaching the Gospel is attributed to them more clearly than any other; for Stephen and Philip devote themselves to an apostolate of the word, accompanied by wonders and exorcisms, and it is precisely this apostolic activity which causes Stephen's arrest and his martyrdom.

Here again the Roman Pontifical has preserved the traditional teaching: "the deacon", says the bishop in his charge, "must serve at the altar, baptize and preach". So, too, Canon 1342 considers preaching as one of the deacon's regular duties. The Fathers of the Church compare deacons to the prophets of the Old Law, or to the seven angels with trumpets described in the Apocalypse, or even to the seven thunders, because their voices echo in the world the very voice of God.

THE SERVICE OF THE PRIESTHOOD

All that has been said about the functions of the deacon can be summed up in a single sentence from the *Apostolic Tradition*: "The deacon is not ordained to the priesthood, but for the service of the bishop, to do as the latter bids him" c. 9). For all the activities of the deacon, the service of the poor, the liturgical service, preaching, are performed only by the direction of the bishop, who retains responsibility even when he provides himself with assistants. In the letters of St Ignatius of Antioch the deacons are always mentioned in close connection with their bishop (*Magnesians* 2. 1; etc.); deacons act as messengers and, in general, regular intermediaries between the bishop and the faithful (*Philad*. 10. 1). So too the Syrian *Didascalia* describes them to us as the mouth, the ear, the heart of the bishop, with whom they are but one (3. 13, 7; 2. 44); they will be approached on routine matters so that the bishop will not be continually interrupted (2. 28); they will be the judges in cases of lesser importance (2. 44). Theirs is a devoted task, a position of confidence, as is stated also by the *Constitution of the Egyptian Church* and by the *Testament of our Lord*. The deacon exercises as well a sort of control over public morals, and accompanies the bishop on his many official tours, as vouched for in the time of Amalar (in his *Liber Officialis*). He is even charged with official missions of the most delicate nature: St Gregory sends the deacon Castorius to inquire into the conduct of bishops and priests (*Letter* 5, 28 and 32).

All these functions naturally put the deacons very much in the public eye and could even give the impression that their ministry was more important than that of simple priests; thus some of them seem to have become puffed up, and there is talk of this as early as St Cyprian (*Letter* 3). To take another example, we know from St Jerome's letter (146) to Evangelus that the Roman deacons had come to consider themselves superior to simple priests.

However, the normal rule is that the deacons are also at the service of these latter, whenever the bishop considers it desirable. The third canon of the Council of Vaison (442) tells us that there was at that time at least a deacon and a subdeacon in each country church entrusted to a priest, and that the latter, when he could not go himself, sent a deacon to fetch the chrism newly consecrated in the episcopal city. In the same way the document known as the *Epistola canonica*, which belongs to the beginning of the sixth century, prescribed in its eighth canon that there should be a deacon with the local priest wherever there are churches with baptismal fonts; the same canon enjoins upon him not only to live in community with the priest but also "not to take up an arrogant attitude towards him". And we find in the *Statuta Ecclesiae antiqua*, an apocryphal work of the fifth century, "the deacon must know that he is servant of the priest as well as of the bishop".

One must not, however, take this last document too seriously, for it has obvious "presbyterian" tendencies: it is the bishop in the first place who is served by the deacons, and if they have to help the simple priest as well it is in the measure in which the latter shares in some way the bishop's authority, takes his place or fulfils his functions when he cannot himself be present.

THE "SACRAMENT" OF THE DIACONATE

If ordination to the diaconate is a true sacramental rite, as Catholic theologians all agree, it must confer a special sacramental grace. Is it possible to state precisely its nature and significance? Christian tradition suggests to us a solution like that which it indicates in regard to priesthood in general: if the sacrament of Order in its higher degrees makes men representatives, signs or sacraments of Christ the priest, the diaconate will be ordained to represent Christ vividly in the Church in the mission which he attributes to himself of serving his Father and serving men.

The texts which demonstrate this aspect of the subject are innumerable: St Ignatius of Antioch bids the faithful of Magnesia honour the deacons as Jesus Christ, for it is the *diakonia* of Christ which has been entrusted to them: we must understand that to mean, as the old Latin version of the fourth century understands it to mean, that the deacons, in regard to the bishop who is the image of the heavenly Father, are "imitators of Christ, because they are the servants of the bishop as Christ is the servant of the Father". This idea is also expressed in the prayer for the ordination of a deacon in the *Apostolic Tradition*: "O God, who has created and ordained everything by your Word, Father of our Lord Jesus Christ, who you have sent to serve your will . . ., grant the spirit of grace, of zeal and of diligence to your servant here present, whom you have chosen to serve your Church and to bring into the holy of holies what has been offered to you by the high priests appointed by you for the glory of your name. . . ."

But if Christ is the deacon, the messenger of the Father, it is to make himself the servant, the *deacon*, of the man whom he comes to save. It is at the solemn moment when he has just given them their commission to offer the eucharistic sacrifice, as his own successors in the priesthood, that Jesus recalls to the apostles, too much inclined to glorify themselves and to behave as masters, his own example as a *deacon*:

> And there was rivalry between them over the question, which of them was to be accounted the greatest. But he told them, The kings of the Gentiles lord it over them, and those who bear rule over them win the name of benefactors. With you it is not to be so; no difference is to be made, among you, between the greatest and the youngest of all, between him who commands and him who serves [literally, who fulfils the office of *deacon*].

And Jesus is not content with this general principle, but refers to his own example: "Tell me, which is greater, the man who sits at table, or the man who serves him? Surely the man who sits at table; yet I am here among you as your servant." To grasp the full import of this last word, we must remember first that Jesus has just distributed the Eucharist to them, but we must find still more in it and read on, remembering that the word *diakonein* means primarily "to prepare the table": "You are the men who have kept to my side in my hours of trial: and, as my Father has allotted a kingdom to me, so I allot to you a place to eat and drink at my table in my kingdom" (Luke 22. 24–30). Thus when Jesus says that he is among his apostles as their servant, it is because he is preparing the table of the eucharistic feast for them, but above all because he is preparing the table of the heavenly feast of which the Eucharist is the sacrament. Had he not said previously: "Blessed are those servants, whom the master will find watching when he comes: I promise you, he will gird himself, and make them sit down to meat, and minister to them" (Luke 12. 37).

The grace special to the diaconate is thus a *charisma*, a spiritual power, fitting a man to serve God and his neighbour, conforming him to Christ who came "to serve and not to be served": the deacons in serving their neighbour are still serving God, as Polycarp of Smyrna reminds them: "The deacons", he wrote, "must be without reproach in the eyes of divine justice, as deacons of God and of Christ who became the deacon of all."

This idea of "service" should make us think also of those other servants of God, the angels; so early Christian writers have seen in the deacons, as ministers at the eucharistic table, the image of the heavenly spirits who are deacons of the heavenly banquet. In a still profounder way we must think, with Hippolytus of Rome, that the deacon, when serving at the altar or when serving the Christian community and its leader, represents once more Christ himself, the angel or messenger of the Father. The Pontifical recalls this traditional title likening the deacon to the angelic powers: "Holy Lord, Father of faith, of hope and of grace, rewarder of good deeds, establisher of the angelic ministry throughout heaven and earth and by it extending the effect of your will to all creatures, deign to adorn your servants here present with a spiritual perfection so that they always obey your commands and grow in purity as they serve your holy altars."

Yet as the priest is not simply a sign of Jesus' priesthood but his instrument whereby the effects of his priesthood are produced, so we must say that the *charisma* of the diaconate makes the deacon not only the representative of Christ who continues to serve his Father and his fellow men, but the instrument of this service; through the deacons, Christ and his grace confer the manifold benefits of which the deacons are the ministers and guarantee the efficacy of their service; that is St Peter's teaching to all those who have received a *charisma* for the service of God's Church: "Make one another free of what is yours ungrudgingly, sharing with all whatever gift each of you has received, as befits the stewards of a God so rich in graces. One of you preaches, let him remember that it is God's message he is uttering; another distributes relief, let him remember that it is God who supplies him the opportunity; that so, in all you do, God may be glorified through Jesus Christ" (1 Peter 4. 10–11).

The grace received on his ordination day thus guarantees the deacon's service an entirely fresh effectiveness in the various fields of his activity.

THE LEVITICAL ORDER

In the Old Testament, apart from Aaron and his sons, God raised up the order of levites for special functions. Ever since Clement of Rome's letter to the Corinthians deacons have been compared to these levites, and the Roman Pontifical once again is only summing up a long tradition when it puts into the mouth of the consecrating bishop the following charges to the ordinands:

> In the Old Law the tribe of Levi was chosen out from the twelve tribes for special dedication to the perpetual service of the Tabernacle and the sacrifices. Its dignity was such that nobody who did not belong to it could pretend to the service of this worship and these functions, so that this peculiar hereditary privilege caused it to be named, and literally to be, the tribe of the Lord. Today, beloved sons,

you are receiving the name and the functions of these
levites, for you also have been chosen to be at the service
of the Tabernacle of Witness, that is of the Church of God,
which is a levitical task. . . . This Church of God, you must
support and defend as a Tabernacle.

We should notice the very characteristic transposition
from the Tabernacle of the desert, which the levites had
to support and defend while the people were on the march,
to the Church which is the new Tabernacle, the place
where God dwells; and this does not refer to our churches
of stone or of wood but to the ecclesiastical society itself.
The importance attached to the deacon's functions is then
clear: this episcopal charge, with which might be compared
the metaphor used by the poet Prudentius (among others)
who compared the deacons with the columns on which
God's altar rests, is a witness to the very considerable
significance attributed to the deacons for many centuries:
the Church's *solidity* depends upon them. This startling
conclusion becomes comprehensible when we remember
their position in the hierarchy: it is by their means that
the bishops accomplish their most difficult and delicate
tasks, in which the hierarchy finds itself in closest contact
with the world and its temporal concerns on the dangerous
frontier between the purely spiritual and the material. The
point will be understood still better if we reflect upon the
qualities which are required of deacons by St Paul.

THE VIRTUES REQUIRED OF DEACONS

They are enumerated in 1 Timothy (3. 8–13): deacons
must be men of decent behaviour. No doubt Polycarp of
Smyrna is making the same stipulation when he requires
deacons to be without reproach. However, in fact a requirement especially of purity, of chastity, has been seen
in this, in accordance with the Latin version of the Vul-

gate, *diaconos similiter pudicos*. This requirement, constantly repeated in our documents about deacons and insisted upon by the Roman Pontifical, is readily understood when we realize that the diaconate involved regular dealings with women, widows and consecrated virgins, and that the ministry of beneficence brought the deacons into close contact with the worst moral as well as physical evils. In the midst of a world which finds it difficult to believe in virtue and does all it can to corrupt it, the deacons must avoid even the appearance of evil.

"They must be men of their word": this requirement of loyalty and sincerity is repeated by the *Didache* in another form: they must be *true*. The Apostle wishes to banish from the lives of deacons falsity and calumny, and all detraction or indiscretion. This too is easily understood if we remember that the deacon acted as a censor of morals on the bishop's behalf: his ministry put him in possession of many secrets and made him acquainted with many delicate situations and hidden sins; his report had to be objective and sincere if the faithful were not to lose confidence in those whose task was to guide and assist them.

"Not given to deep drinking or to money getting": in the midst of the manifold occasions which his function itself created for him, the deacon has to remember that the goods and supplies for which he is responsible are not his own, but the patrimony of the poor: charged as he is with preparing the bread and wine for the Eucharist and with the distributions to the needy, he might be tempted to put aside a generous share of it for his own use, or for that of his family, imitating the servant in the parable "eating and drinking himself drunk" as he waits for his master's return (Luke 12. 45). These diaconal tasks could tempt the clergy by the "seduction of riches", with all the familiar evils which result therefore for the Church; from the time of the *Didache* and Polycarp the Christian conscience

constantly requires the clergy engaged in these diaconal
tasks not to "love money".

"Keeping true, in all sincerity of conscience, to the faith
that has been revealed": it is not altogether easy to determine with certainty the exact significance of this Pauline
expression; in the parallel enumeration of the qualities
required of the deaconess, it corresponds to the simple
quality of faithfulness, one of the traditional virtues of
good servants; in any case, faithfulness is certainly required of the deacon: one must be able to rely upon him
in full security, to put confidence in him. However, St
Paul's expression seems to have a further bearing: it is
indeed a question of faithfulness but in regard to the pre-
servation of the mysteries of the Gospel of which the
deacons are, in a measure, the dispensers. As intermediaries
between the priesthood and the faithful they must possess
and transmit intact the deposit which they have received.

THE DECADENCE OF THE DIACONATE

We have seen that the deacon had a very important
position in the early centuries of the Church's history: as
personal assistant to the bishop, controller of ecclesiastical
goods, private secretary, major-domo of God's house, he
often seemed more important than the simple priest. Often,
too, the bishop's successor was chosen from among the
deacons and during a vacancy it was the archdeacon who
acted as administrator. Again the deacons often had a predominant influence in the Councils of the Church: Atha-
nasius was still only a deacon when he assisted at the
Council of Nicaea and played a leading part in it; Hilary
too, whom Leo the Great sent as his legate to the Council
of Ephesus in 449 and who succeeded him on the throne
of St Peter. Pope Pelagius II sends the future Gregory the
Great, while still a deacon, as his ambassador to Constan-

tinople. As late as the eleventh century Hildebrand is only archdeacon of the Church of Rome when he is sent as ambassador to the Emperor.

We have also seen that the deacons sometimes tended to abuse their prerogatives; the Councils of Arles and Nicaea in the fourth century intervened to reform these abuses, and in particular to restrain the deacons' tendency to oppose the authority of simple priests in rural parishes.

For rural parishes in which the bishop did not regularly reside (the Council of Arles of 314 is our best authority for the beginnings of this transformation) were gradually coming into being at this time; what was to be the position of the deacon, who is traditionally the assistant to the bishop, in these parishes? Since the Mass could not be celebrated without a deacon (this remained the rule until much later), the priest of a parish, however small, needed his presence. Moreover, these parishes gradually acquired independent exchequers; this was the rule, according to Imbart de la Tour, for Gaul and Africa by the second half of the fifth century. Henceforth, each church could have its own clergy, recruited from the locality and attached to the service of the local church.

Deacons seem to have played a very important part in this extension of the church to the smallest centres: they often founded small local communities and presided over them in their earliest stages until such time as they received a priest: Cyril of Jerusalem, in his seventeenth *Catechesis*, and St Jerome in his *Dialogue against the Luciferians*, refer to Christians in remote places who have been baptized by deacons. Students of Irish monasticism have shown that it was the custom of St Patrick and of St Martin to place small centres of worship under the control of a deacon. Canon 77 of the Council of Elvira, about the year 300, already speaks of the *diaconus regens populum* (the deacon in charge of the people). These deacons, of course, were often married, could not celebrate the Eucharist, but they could distribute it, preside over meetings for prayer, preach, baptize, settle the innumerable questions which arose, organize the service of beneficence and of assistance for the poor and prepare catechumens for baptism.

In our time, on the other hand, the diaconate, at least in the west, is only a temporary office, a stepping stone on the way to the priesthood. How has this come about? One might suppose that the introduction and general adoption of private Masses, in the west, made people feel that the diaconate, as a permanent office, had lost its justification.

According to W. Schamoni, we must find a further reason for this in the modifications of the status of the clergy which can be traced as far back as the Apostolic Canons, a collection put together about the year 400; Canon 41 instructs the bishop to make his clergy live by the altar, and soon after this clerics are forbidden to work with their hands for their livelihood. In certain times of stringency resources must have been greatly reduced and this would have led to a reduction in the number of beneficiaries; the deacons would have been the first to go. Finally, the prohibition of marriage, or at least of its use, having been extended to deacons—traces of this can be found at the time of the Council of Elvira (the beginning of the fourth century)—recruitment for this order became still more difficult.

There may be also a deeper reason for the change: the theology of Order in the west concentrated more and more on the sacramental powers conferred, in particular on the powers relating to the Eucharist, leaving in the shade the spiritual *charisma*, or considering the grace conferred by it only as an increase of sanctifying grace. Now the diaconate, strictly speaking, does not confer any sacramental power conditioning the valid administration of any sacrament; so the importance attached to this institution was necessarily diminished. Further, if the grace conferred by the sacrament is considered primarily as an increase of sanctifying grace, that is of the personal sanctification of the recipient, and not as a spiritual enablement to perform certain services in the community and for the good of the community (*charisma*), a deacon, provided that he had the necessary qualifications, would actually desire to receive the increase of interior personal sanctification which the priesthood would give him. Thus a permanent deacon might easily appear a retarded or unworthy person.

Whatever the reasons, the diaconate is only a temporary office in the west today. Diaconal tasks are performed by priests and some of them by laymen. In spite of the desire expressed by the Council of Trent in Canon 17 of its decree (on the reform of order), the link between the priesthood and the Christian people, which was once contributed by the diaconate and the minor orders, has practically disappeared.

CHAPTER V

THE ORDERS BELOW THE

DIACONATE

In *The Apostolic Tradition* in addition to bishops, priests
and deacons, Hippolytus of Rome mentions lectors and
subdeacons: the latter are described as assisting the deacon;
and Hippolytus makes it clear that they are not *ordained*
in the strict sense of the term any more than widows,
virgins or those who have the gift of healing.

This is the historical origin of the problem about the
orders lower than the diaconate. The list of them has varied
a great deal, and a detailed study of these variations would
be of little interest; whereas in the east there are only two
orders, the subdiaconate and the lectorate, in the west there
are today the five minor orders enumerated by Pope Cornelius, about the year 251, in a letter (fragmentarily preserved by Eusebius) to Bishop Fabius of Antioch against
the proceedings of Novatian: "Did Novatian not know
then that there must be only one bishop in a Catholic
Church? In this church [i.e. the Roman] he was not
ignorant—how could he have been?—that there are
forty-six priests, seven deacons, forty-two acolytes,
fifty-two exorcists, lectors and door keepers."

What is the significance of these ordinations, these
orders, of which the New Testament makes no mention?

Can they be considered as really forming part of the sacrament of Order? How were these various degrees brought into the Church? These are the questions which we must briefly consider.

THE FUNCTIONS OF THE SUBDEACON

The phrase in the *Apostolic Constitutions* (8) defining the subdeacons as the "servants of the deacons", summarizes the findings of history. Mgr Duchesne, in his study of the origins of Christian worship, reaches the conclusion that the functions of the subdeacon are simply a development of the deacon's.

The latter, weighed down by cares of every kind, must have soon felt the need to obtain assistance from Christians of good will; these, who must have been originally simple laymen, received later a special blessing when they were given their commission: from that sprang the subdiaconate. The functions which we find them performing are in fact those of the deacon: the *Apostolic Constitutions* describe them as helping the deacons to watch over the door of the church, busying themselves with the sacred vessels and assisting in the service of the altar. The letters of St Gregory the Great reveal another aspect of their activity which also belongs to the deacon's sphere: they sometimes administer the Church's patrimony, conduct inquiries, give judgement in the name of the pope, and sit with bishops on ecclesiastical tribunals.

Liturgical documents naturally concentrate on their functions during the celebration of the Eucharist: here again it is clear that the subdeacons are the assistants of the deacons: according to the oldest Roman *Ordo*, after helping the bishop to vest and accompanying him to the altar, they help the deacons to remove their chasubles and put themselves at their disposal for the rest of the ceremony. So too the third Roman *Ordo* shows the subdeacon accompanying the archdeacon and assisting him in his duties.

To perform their office at the altar the subdeacons were naturally given the right to touch the vessels and the sacred cloths; and it was their business to wash them.

These are the functions which the present Roman Pontifical lists in the bishop's charge to candidates for the subdiaconate: "At the moment of receiving the office of subdeacon, dearly beloved brethren, consider carefully what ministry is committed to you. The subdeacon must prepare water for the service of the altar, serve the deacon, wash the cloths and the corporals, present to the deacon the chalice and the paten which are used for the sacrifice."

Other functions could be mentioned: according to the same liturgical document, the subdeacon has the responsibility for distributing the offerings made by the faithful; and we know from St Gregory the Great that subdeacons sometimes took the place of deacons as cantors.

In short, we receive a clear impression that the subdeacon was originally simply a deputy or even a servant of the deacon, doing part of his work, under his authority and superintendence, and without receiving a true ordination which would give him a share in the sacrament of order.

THE SUBDIACONATE AS A MAJOR ORDER

It is certain that, in the first centuries of the Church, the subdiaconate was not considered a sacramental rite or even an order properly so called: this is perfectly clear in Hippolytus, who does not allow the subdeacon the imposition of hands, which is reserved for the clergy. Even when this latter rite was introduced into the ceremony at installing a subdeacon, it was never considered, at any rate

in the east, as a participation in a sacrament instituted by
God but as a simple sacramental instituted by the Church.

In the Latin Church this does not remain the only view:
gradually as the diaconate began to be considered as only
a stage towards the priesthood, the subdiaconate approxi-
mated to the diaconate. Alexander II (1061–73) enumerates
three sacred orders, the priesthood, the diaconate and the
subdiaconate. But it seems that this terminology was not
accepted everywhere, since in 1901 the Council of Benevento prescribed: "Henceforth nobody shall be chosen as
bishop unless he has lived devoutly in sacred orders. By
sacred orders, we mean the diaconate, and the priesthood.
For, according to the witness of Scripture, there are only
two orders which the primitive Church possessed: for them
alone we have the apostles' mandate." These words of the
Council of Benevento are almost exactly repeated by
Hugh of St Victor and Peter Lombard. Towards the end
of the twelfth century, Peter the Cantor declares that subdeacons should not receive the imposition of hands and
that it is a novelty to consider the subdiaconate a sacred
order. But a decree attributed to Innocent III, bearing the
date 1207 and found in Gregory IX's collection, puts an
end to the discussion and causes the subdiaconate in the
west to be considered as a major order.

The liturgy itself has retained traces of this evolution:
with the eighth century a tendency is found in France to
anticipate the charge previously given to the deacons before the ordination of subdeacons; so it was not long before
the litanies of the Saints and the prostration were also
anticipated, despite the contrary usage, preserved in the
Papal Pontifical until the fifteenth century, of keeping the
prostration for the deacon and ordaining the subdeacons
only after the communion along with the other minor
orders.

THE OBLIGATION OF CELIBACY

The tendency to assimilate the subdiaconate to the diaconate seems easy to explain when we remind ourselves again that the theology of Order, in the west, came gradually to put the powers conferred in the forefront, and not the special sacramental grace: in fact, the subdeacon, in helping the deacon, performed practically all the latter's functions, and so seemed to have practically the same powers; why, then, should there be such a difference between the two ordinations?

Another fact too must be taken into account: very early, again in the Latin Church, the obligations of deacons began to be imposed upon subdeacons, in particular the obligation of continence, which is mentioned as early as the Council of Carthage in 401. The popes, however, do not seem to have forbidden them the use of marriage until St Leo who, in his fourteenth letter, forbids it absolutely: "Those who have a wife must be as though they had none, those who have none must remain colibate."

This prohibition is gradually extended to the other dioceses during the fifth and sixth centuries; at the end of the sixth century the subdeacons of Sicily still did not consider themselves absolutely bound in this way, despite a special intervention by Pelagius II in 587. St Gregory the Great had to deal with them on several occasions, and also the subdeacons of Reggio: in the end he allowed those who were already married to use their conjugal rights, but decreed that in future only those were to be admitted to this order who had made up their minds to observe continence.

As the Council of the Lateran (1123) had declared null all marriages contracted by clerks in major orders, the subdiaconate, which became a major order in the course of the twelfth century, fell under this ruling; it was perpetuated and the Code of Canon Law maintains it to this day: "Clerks in major orders cannot contract marriage, and their obligation to observe chastity is such that in sinning against this virtue they also commit a sacrilege" (Can. 132).

If we add to this obligation that of the daily recitation of the Breviary, it is easy to see why in our time the subdiaconate, rather than the diaconate, appears the most important and decisive step in the preparation for the priesthood.

THE ORDER OF ACOLYTES

Nevertheless this step, in the Latin Church, is preceded by several others: before becoming a subdeacon, a man must have been an acolyte, an exorcist, a lector, a doorkeeper, and before receiving these minor orders, he must have received the tonsure.

Acolyte means follower, and this is the word used by the *Liber Pontificalis* in reference to Pope Gaius (283–96): "The latter (Pope Gaius) laid it down that the sequence of order in the Church should be the following: if a man is to become a bishop, he must first be doorkeeper, lector, exorcist, *follower* (*sequens*), subdeacon, deacon, priest, and only then may he be ordained bishop." Acolytes are first mentioned in the middle of the third century in the letter of St Cornelius to Fabius of Antioch, already quoted, about the proceedings of Novatian: in Rome, at this time, there were forty-two of them, and it seems clear that their number was equally large at Carthage, to judge from the frequency with which they are mentioned in St Cyprian's letters.

St Cyprian informs us of their functions: they are employed as *tabellarii* (secretaries), as the bishop's messengers or couriers; but they were not only entrusted with confidential messages, as certain well-known facts make clear: the acolyte Tarsicius was martyred for refusing to hand over to the pagans the Eucharist which he had been instructed to take to the absent brethren; according to Innocent I's letter to Decentius of Gubbio (416), on each Sunday acolytes carried to the priest of the secondary churches the bread consecrated by the pope, the *fermentum*; in the sixth century John the Deacon, in a letter to Senarius, distinguishes the acolytes from the exorcists precisely by their privilege of carrying the "sacraments" and presenting them to the priests: this last detail is illustrated by an old Roman *Ordo* which describes the acolytes as wearing round their necks a linen bag for the consecrated loaves to be divided for the communion of the faithful; furthermore, the ceremony of their ordination consists in the bestowal of this little bag.

In Rome they also carry the sacred chrism, and an *Ordo* of the seventh century makes this an obligation for them: "The acolyte must never be without the chrism so that, if he accompanies the bishop and the latter wishes to administer confirmation, he may be always ready to perform his office." This text is all the more interesting as making clear what an acolyte originally was, a *follower* of the bishop.

So we are again witnessing a splitting up of the deacon's tasks, for all that has been described once belonged to him; occupied by other cares, the deacon could not be always at the bishop's disposal; they attached to themselves collaborators who were charged with this duty, reliable men who were later commissioned with a special ceremony.

But, as one would expect, the decline of the deacon's importance involved a corresponding decline in that of the acolyte, who was soon confined to certain liturgical functions: looking after the lights, the "porrection" (presentation) of the wine and water at the altar. The present rite of ordination for acolytes, substantially the same as that found in the collection known as *Statuta Ecclesiae antiqua* (belonging to the end of the fifth century or the beginning of the sixth), consists in making them touch a candlestick with a candle and an empty cruet, while the bishop pronounces a corresponding formula.

In our time the office of acolyte has remained a step towards the priesthood; although its functions are nearly always fulfilled by laymen, sacristans or Mass-servers, and although the desire expressed by the Council of Trent in its twenty-third session is still unanswered, the Church continues to extend to her future priests a solemn invitation to a life more worthy of the service of the altar.

THE ORDER OF EXORCISTS

We must come to the same conclusion, and even more definitely, about the office of exorcist, which has no function of its own in the Church, not even that which its name implies.

The word exorcist, used for the first time in the Acts of the Apostles (19. 13), refers to one who adjures a demon to leave a place, or a person, and has the power to drive him out.

In the earliest days of Christianity, the power of exorcism belonged more or less to all Christians or was a personal *charisma* granted by God to individuals, apart from an intervention by the hierarchy: it is probably this latter case which Hippolytus of Rome has in mind when he writes in the *Apostolic Tradition*: "If anyone seems to have received the *gift of healing* by revelation, hands should not be laid upon him, since the matter is made clear."

This gift of healing, which many consider to be the gift

of delivering the possessed, was not, therefore, given by a
special order: it was thought sufficient to prove that the
charisma had been received.

On the other hand it is difficult not to give the word
exorcist a more official sense, when Pope Cornelius
enumerates the exorcists, along with the door-keepers and
lectors, making them fifty-two in all for the city of Rome.
About the same time a letter addressed to Cornelius and
found in his correspondence (n. 23) ends with the following
note by the scribe: "I, Lucian, have written this letter, in
the presence of two members of the clergy: an exorcist
and a lector." It seems, then, that by the third century, in
Rome and in Africa, exorcists formed an order of their
own in the clergy of these two churches. But it has not been
so everywhere, and in the east it does not seem that the
exorcists ever constituted a special order.

The *Statuta Ecclesiae antiqua* again give us our first in-
formation, in Canon 95, about a special "ordination" for
exorcists; the rite is that prescribed by the present Roman
Pontifical: the bishop gives the ordinand the book containing the prayers of exorcism, saying to him: "Take
(these exorcisms), engrave them on your memory and
receive the power to lay hands on those who are possessed
by the demon whether baptized or catechumens."

We must therefore suppose that the exorcists were
originally clerics who were regularly charged with pro-
nouncing the "exorcisms" over the "energumens". It has
been thought that the bishop, to whom this function belonged in the first instance, began by employing substitutes
to recite the prayers of exorcism over the catechumens,
during the service of Christian initiation and that the privilege was later extended to the exorcisms over the possessed,
properly so called. This function must have devolved in
the first place upon priests or deacons: in Hippolytus of
Rome, a priest presides over the abjurations of the cate-

chumens and their unction with exorcised oil, carried by a deacon; at Milan, according to St Ambrose's account in the *De sacramentis*, a levite, that is, a deacon, receives the candidates' renunciation of Satan at baptism.

We know too that the "energumens" were looked after by the deacons during the celebration of the holy mysteries; St John Chrysostom tells us that a deacon introduced the demoniacs into the church and told them to bow their heads; this duty, like that of keeping the unworthy from the Holy Table, must often have been entrusted also to exorcists.

But in 416 Pope Innocent I reserved the exorcism properly so called, that is, of the possessed, to priests and deacons. The first editions of the Roman Ritual, starting in 1614, still allow for the priest's being replaced by another exorcist, but the later editions, subsequent to the Code of Canon Law, speak only of the priest: moreover the latter must have received a special and express authorization from his ordinary to perform his task.

What, then, remains for the exorcists if their chief function, indicated by their name, is henceforth suspended? According to the Roman Pontifical, they retain a certain power to keep away the unworthy, or rather, to keep away if need be those who are not communicating so that access to the Holy Table may be unimpeded. These humble functions at least symbolize to some extent the office of purification, of discrimination, which once belonged to the exorcist; today, once more, laymen perform it, and the office of exorcist, in practice, confers no special power in the Church; but this order continues to remind future priests of the necessity for fighting against the wiles of the demon and against sin in all its forms.

THE ORDER OF LECTORS

Early evidence is far more plentiful about the lectors: and this order is the only "lower" one, except the sub-diaconate, which is accepted both by east and west.

The origin of this function is comprehensible enough: we have only to read St Justin's account, in his first *Apology*, of the Sunday assemblies: "On the day called the day of the Sun, there is an assembly of all those who live in the towns or in the country. The memoirs of the Apostles are read, or the writings of the prophets, according to the length of time available. Then, when the lector has finished, the president speaks, exhorting the people and encouraging them to virtuous conduct."

There is nothing to show that this lector is a member of the clergy, but his function is plain; before the bishop's exhortation, it is his duty to read aloud the passage of Scripture on which the latter is to comment. In fact this was another diaconal function; but the deacon might need an assistant or a substitute for this task, and Christians specially qualified to read and articulate clearly were naturally chosen for the purpose.

By the time of Hippolytus, in any case, the lectorate has become a separate institution, although its members were not yet strictly a part of the clergy, since they received no true ordination: "the lector is appointed by the reception of the book from the bishop, for he is not ordained."

During this period mortuary inscriptions often mention lectors, but add little to our knowledge of this order. But in St Cyprian's writings a development is brought to our notice, for he considers the lectors as forming part of the clergy and as receiving a true "ordination": "Since it is necessary for my letters to be carried by clerics [he wrote to his clergy], and since many of them are absent and the few who remain are not enough for day-to-day require-

ments, I have had to 'ordain' some new ones for the
purpose. Know, then, that I have ordained Saturus lector,
and Optatus the confessor subdeacon."

This testimony from St Cyprian's twenty-ninth letter
must be compared with the moving account in the thirty-
eighth letter of the youthful Aurelius who had twice publicly confessed his faith under the torture of persecution:

> Such a young man would deserve the higher degrees of
> clerical ordination, if not by reason of his years, at least by
> reason of his merits. However, for the time being, I have
> thought it right to begin by making him a lector. For
> nothing better befits a voice which has confessed God in a
> profession of glorious faith than to pronounce the divine
> writings in public reading, and, after uttering the sublime
> words which have given testimony to Christ, to read the
> Gospel of Christ, from which the witness of the martyrs
> derives, to come to the ambo after going to the pillory. . . .
> Know, then, dearly beloved brethren, that he has been
> ordained by me and by those of our colleagues who were
> present.

These lines of St Cyprian's not only explain to us the
nature of the lector's functions but also inform us that
they were sometimes fulfilled by adolescents. On the evidence of a long inscription which is perhaps the epitaph
of Liberius (352–6) it has even been thought that there
were sometimes quite young children in the ranks of the
lectors. Mgr Duchesne writes: "Their silvery voices pene-
trated the vast spaces of the basilicas and carried to the
furthest rows of the assembly. In a task so weighty for
those of so tender an age they were tempted to mischief."

And in fact the inscription just mentioned congratulated
the deceased, who had been a lector in his childhood, on
always fulfilling his task with gravity and piety, without
yielding to the temptation of "jumping a page" for fun.
These little details are not surprising when we remember

that Pope Siricius, in 385, in a letter to the bishop of Tarragona, approves and indeed prescribes admitting to the
position of lector children who had not reached the age
of puberty: the youthfulness of these clerics did, however,
create serious problems, and it is understandable that the
Scholae Lectorum which are found in various churches
were required for their training and instruction.

The functions of the lectors were not confined to reading; they were entrusted also with the performance of certain chants. In his account of the Vandal persecution, about
the year 490, Victor, Bishop of Vita, relates the following
incident: "One Easter Day, about 470, a lector of Aegia
was in the pulpit chanting Alleluia when a troop of armed
Arians tried to get into the church. Finding the doors
locked, they climbed the walls and shot arrows through
the windows; one of them pierced the lector's throat, he
dropped the book and died."

When the reading of Scripture was reduced to the
Epistle and Gospel of the Mass, entrusted to the deacon
and subdeacon respectively, the function proper to the
lector lost its importance, and that of chanter became
primary: the *Schola Lectorum* had been turned into the
Schola Cantorum by the seventh century.

During the persecutions of the first centuries the lectors
often had another responsibility directly connected with
their principal function, that of keeping safe the Holy
Books. This was not a sinecure, since during certain persecutions, particularly that of Diocletian, there was a tendency to seize and destroy copies of Sacred Scriptures.

Very little is left today of these various functions, although the texts of the Pontifical still echo a situation
which long ago ceased to exist; the lector's function of
reading the Scripture is practically reduced to the right to
sing the lessons during the solemn celebration of the night
Office: and even so no prescription confines this right to

the lectors. Canon 1147 reduces the faculty of "blessing bread and the new fruits" explicitly affirmed by the Pontifical to "benedictions expressly mentioned by the Code"; now the Code does not mention any, and in practice only the priest gives these blessings. However, the office of lector still reminds us of the place which the reading of Scripture ought to have in the life of every priest and of his obligation of conforming his life to it.

THE ORDER OF DOORKEEPERS

In the east there is often mention of doorkeepers; according to the *Apostolic Constitutions*, they were employed to guard the entrance to the men's side of the church. But they were not counted as members of the clergy.

In the west doorkeepers do not often appear in our surviving documents; after Pope St Cornelius, who notices them along with the exorcists and the lectors, they are mentioned by the third Council of Carthage in 397; the Fathers, in Canon 21, prescribe that they must be considered members of the clergy. However, Pope Siricius, writing to Himerius of Tarragona on February 10th, 385, and giving him directions about promotion to various degrees in the clerical body, makes no mention of doorkeepers. Nor does Pope Zosimus. Pope Gelasius does mention them in a document of 494, but only to contrast their office, which can be filled by the uneducated, with the orders of the clergy, which require a certain knowledge of letters. In fact, we find no rite of ordination mentioned even by way of allusion until the *Statuta Ecclesiae antiqua* about the beginning of the sixth century; the rite in the present Pontifical is derived from this Gallican document.

The functions of doorkeepers are those indicated by their name; opening and shutting the doors of the church and the sacristy, keeping away the unworthy, keeping a check on those who enter, ringing bells to announce the liturgical offices, preparing the book of the Gospels for the preacher. These are, in fact, the duties which are performed nowadays by sacristans; in entrusting them solemnly to her future priests the Church declares the dignity of everything that has to do with divine worship.

ARE THE LOWER ORDERS SACRAMENTAL?

Thus from the subdiaconate to the office of doorkeeper there are five degrees through which the candidate to the priesthood has to pass on his way to the diaconate. What is to be thought of them in relation to the sacrament of order?

Medieval scholastic theologians generally allow that all the orders have a share in the sacrament of Order; most of the canonists belonging to the same period say the opposite; and there have always been some theologians who consider minor orders as mere sacramentals, in particular Durandus of Saint Pourçain in the fourteenth century who, with the fine resolution which characterizes him, did not hesitate to reduce the sacrament of Order to the priesthood alone, excluding even the diaconate.

As historical research, especially since the Council of Trent, revealed the fluctuations and uncertainties which have always attended the subject, theologians have more and more abandoned the position held by the principal theologians of the Middle Ages.

No valid argument seems to support the latter's position. To be a sacrament an institution must go back to Christ himself; and not only is there no trace of this institution in the New Testament, but the successive appearances of these various lower degrees at very irregular intervals in the Church's history makes it clear enough that they were instituted, as necessity arose, by the Church herself.

During the discussions on the subject which took place at the Council of Trent, the Fathers refused to entertain any suggestion in favour of the opinion, although widespread at the time, which defended the sacramentality of the lower orders.

Without seeing in it an absolutely decisive argument against this view, one may nevertheless attach great significance to the fact that Pius XII, in the Constitution *Sacramentum Ordinis* of November 30th, 1947, considers only the episcopate, the priesthood and the diaconate; further, in putting an end to the discussions about the rite essential to the sacrament and in excluding from this the delivery of the instruments, this document removes any appearance of probability from an opinion which considers as sacramental orders to which no delivery of instruments is attributed—and no imposition of hands signifying the bestowal of a grace.

It has been pointed out, nevertheless, that these lower orders are never repeated, which would seem to indicate that they confer an indelible character and therefore that they are sacraments; the obvious reply to this is that many of the Church's benedictions are conferred only once upon the person without making anyone suppose that they are sacraments, such as the blessing of an abbess, or the consecration of a virgin and especially the tonsure, the sacramental on which something must now be said in concluding this chapter on the minor orders.

THE TONSURE

A very old custom, in force among the pagans themselves, considered the offering of a tuft of hair to a divinity or important personage a mark of honour or a sign of submission to this divinity or this personage. In the fourth book of the Aeneid, Dido, when dying, offers Pluto a lock of hair to obtain his protection. In the Middle Ages many instances are known of such offerings of hair to highly placed persons; according to Paul the Deacon in his History of the Lombards, Charles Martel sent his son Pepin to offer a piece of his hair to King Liutprand.

So it is not surprising that the Church took over this symbolic gesture for religious purposes: the old sacramentaries contain special blessings for children or adults who perform it; furthermore, Simeon of Thessalonica, in the fifteenth century, knows of a tonsure received by small children during the ceremony of their baptism.

St Paul said to the Corinthians (1 Cor. 11. 14): "Does not nature itself teach you that it is a disgrace to a man to wear his hair long?" Possibly it was this remark which led monks and clerics from the earliest times to wear their hair very short; in any case, as Thomassin well showed, and despite an opinion very widespread in the Middle Ages, there is no ground for claiming that the tonsure was officially instituted by St Peter.

Gradually the clergy acquired the habit of leaving a crown of hair round the head, as we see in many Roman mosaics and frescoes, and this is the tonsure known in the Middle Ages as the *"tonsure of St Peter"*. The crown, however, varied in size in different countries: Canon 41 of the Fourth Council of Toledo contains this significant prescription: "All clerics and lectors, like deacons and priests, must have the tops of their heads shaved, leaving only a circular crown below; they must not do as lectors in the regions of Gaul seem to have done hitherto and wear their hair long like laymen, cutting off only a small circle on top of the head."

Monks, however, continued to wear the big tonsure, that is, to shave the whole head, and that is what the Venerable Bede, among other writers, calls the "tonsure of St Paul", which remained in use also among the Greek clergy.

The Celts claimed to have a special tonsure going back to St John, which the Romans called derisively the "tonsure of Simon Magus"; they kept their hair long at the back of the head and shaved all the front part from ear to ear, apart from a very small half-crown above the forehead; this custom disappears in the eighth or ninth century, after painful discussions, traces of which are found in Bede's *Ecclesiastical History*.

After the year 1000, the rule became general for all the clergy, and councils frequently refer to it: the Council of Worcester, in 1240, adds a detail which deserves mention: "They must not let their hair grow, but must be properly shaven all round the head, keeping only a crown of hair *of the size suitable to the order which they have received*": this matter of the size appropriate to the different orders is the subject of many particular prescriptions by local councils.

But it is not easy to decide when a special ceremony for the tonsure was introduced; according to the Greek monk Cyril of Scythopolis, who wrote a life of St Euthymius in the sixth century, the latter received the tonsure in 379 from the bishop of Mitylene, when he gave him the lectorate. It appears to have been the rule for a long time that the tonsure was given at the reception of the first order. However, in 458, Caesarius, the future bishop of Arles, asked his bishop Sylvester to make him a cleric of his church *ablatis sibi capillis, mutatoque habitu* (cutting his hair and giving him the habit).

The sacramentary of Gellone, which furnishes evidence of the Gelasian sacramentary of the eighth century, mentions a special and distinct rite for giving the tonsure, with corresponding prayers; the ceremony consisted simply in cutting the hair. To this rite Durandus of Mende adds later the giving of the *cotta*, the modern surplice, and the two ceremonies are substantially preserved in our present Roman Pontifical.

Today it is the ceremony of the tonsure which makes a layman into a cleric; this prescription of Canon 108 is completed by the following canons which determine the obligations and privileges of clerics. But henceforth, as with minor orders, a candidate is not admitted unless he has the intention of going on to the priesthood. Thus the tonsure is the first official step on the way to becoming a priest, and this is profoundly significant, since it makes a separation from the world and a total consecration to the service of God; the priest by his vocation is set apart, separated from the rest of men, as Cardinal Suhard wrote: "The first word which accompanies his first move on the way to the priesthood is a spiritual testament: he renounces the world and chooses God: *Dominus pars hereditatis meae* —God is the lot of his heritage."

CHAPTER VI

THE CELIBACY OF THE
CLERGY

Pius XI, in his encyclical *Ad Catholici sacerdotii fastigium* of December 20th, 1935, wrote:

> The light of reason alone can discern an indubitable connection between the virtue of chastity and the sacerdotal ministry: since God is a Spirit, it is appropriate that he who consecrates himself to his service should be in some sort "despoiled of his body". The ancient Romans had glimpsed this appropriateness. One of their most ancient laws which commands them "to approach the gods chastely" is cited by their greatest orator with the comment: "The law ordains that we should approach the gods chastely, that is, with a chastity of the soul, in which everything is contained; it does not exclude chastity of the body, but it must be understood that, since the soul is superior to the body, in order to preserve the body's purity, that of the soul must be preserved even more" (Cicero, *De legibus*, 2, 8).

Obviously there can be no question of denying that purity befits a priest, just as it befits him to acquire all the virtues or at least to aim at them. But this is not only a matter of purity, for this virtue is required of every Christian, single or married. There is a requirement special to the very condition of being a priest which demands of those called to this state a total abstention from the intercourse permitted to those in the state of marriage, and this is known as perfect chastity.

It should be remarked at once that exceptions to this requirement are not ruled out, and the Church has always realized this; in our own day it authorizes certain of its priests, especially in the eastern Churches, to make use of their conjugal rights if they were married before their ordination. So this cannot be more than a matter of supreme appropriateness which the Church has thought it desirable to make obligatory, for the common good of the Church, upon the great majority of her priests.

This requirement has been so often misunderstood that it will be useful to consider its bases and to trace its origins.

ADUMBRATIONS IN THE OLD TESTAMENT

A certain requirement of chastity can already be seen in the prescription of the Old Testament about priests: for the period of their consecration, seven days, Aaron and his sons had to stay in the Tabernacle day and night, and so to practise continence (Lev. 8. 33–5). An incident in the First Book of Samuel adds a further detail: David, coming to the priest Achimelech at Nob, asks for a little bread for his party; since there was nothing but consecrated bread, the priest consented to give it "provided that the men have kept themselves from the touch of woman"; since this bread was normally reserved for the priests, it seems to follow that these had to abstain from intercourse with their wives in order to eat it.

However, it has to be remembered that Judaism before the time of Christ commonly considered marriage as a duty and had nothing but scorn for the celibate or the sterile; eunuchs were excluded from liturgical assemblies.

Yet a passage from the third part of Isaias, the importance of which has been emphasized by Karl Barth, indicates that in the messianic era there was a different outlook:

> Keep right order, the Lord says, faithful to your duty still; ere long I will send deliverance, my own faithfulness shall be revealed. Blessed, every man that so lives, every mother's son that by this rule holds fast, keeps the sabbath holy, and his own hands clear of mischief. Proselyte let him be, of alien birth, will the Lord deny him citizenship? Eunuch let him be, is he no better than a barren trunk, cut down as worthless? Nay, for yonder eunuch the Lord has this message: Who keeps my sabbath? Who makes my will his choice, true to my covenant? A place he shall have in this house, within these walls of mine a memorial; son nor daughter his name could so perpetuate; such a memorial I will grant him as time shall never efface (Isaias 56. 1–5).

This promise suggests the coming of a new order in which sterility—voluntary or otherwise—will no longer be a disgrace and there will be room for voluntary celibacy with a spiritual fecundity more precious than that of the body.

We know, in fact, that the finer spirits among the Jews had grasped the possibility of this even before the coming of Jesus. Among the Rabbis there is the case of Ben Azzai who would never marry, and who said: "My soul rests entirely upon the Law: thus I have no time for marriage; the world can be kept going by others." But especially noteworthy is the case of the Essenes, of whom Pliny tells us that they did not marry and that they practised perfect continence; there was indeed, according to the Jewish historian Josephus, a class of Essenes who married—even so, with very strict rules of continence—but the majority of them renounced marriage altogether; the same author goes on to insist that there was in this no disapproval of marriage and its legitimate use: the purpose of abstinence seems to have been, as Philo says, to have time for a more perfect living of the common life: "He who is held by his wife's charms, naturally takes care of himself and not of others."

THE EXAMPLE OF CHRIST

Born of a Virgin, Christ did not know marriage or the love of the flesh. Apart from all other reasons, there is here an indication which could not be overlooked by Christians, especially those who wished to imitate their master in the most perfect way.

But Jesus does not oblige all to follow this example. He seems indeed to declare that a particular vocation is necessary for this, a special grace which is not given to all: his disciples, we read, when he had spoken to them of the indissolubility of marriage, were dismayed at these demands: "At this, his disciples said to him, If the case stands so between man and wife, it is better not to marry at all. That conclusion, he said, cannot be taken in by everybody, but only by those who have the gift. There are some eunuchs who were so born from the mother's womb, some were made so by men, and some have made themselves so for the love of the kingdom of heaven; take this in, you whose hearts are large enough for it" (Matt. 19. 10–12).

Thus there is a voluntary celibacy undertaken for the Kingdom of God which is accepted by Jesus, and even encouraged by him, a special grace which is not received by everyone. Christ must have been thinking not only of himself and of Mary and Joseph but also of John the Baptist: he too knew no earthly marriage, but spoke the words preserved for us in St John's Gospel, significant for our purpose: "I am not the Christ; I have been sent to go before him. The bride is for the bridegroom, but the bridegroom's friend, who stands by and listens to him, rejoices

too, rejoices at hearing the bridegroom's voice; and this joy
is mine now in full measure" (John 3. 28–9).

St John the Baptist's joy is not in human love; sent to
announce the coming of the Bridegroom, his vocation has
entirely absorbed him, and he cannot think of preparing
for any marriage save that of the Lamb, or of finding any
joy save that of seeing his imminent coming.

These words of his can certainly enlighten us on the
celibacy of Jesus himself: he, as we know, came to
announce and to prepare for the coming of the Kingdom:
and this Kingdom is often described by Jesus as a marriage
feast with the Son of God as the Bridegroom and the
Church as the Bride (Apoc. 19. 7; 21. 2); how then could
he have any other betrothed, any other spouse, here on
earth? How could he have failed to inaugurate during his
earthly life that future life of all God's children which he
describes to the Sadducees in such striking terms: "The
children of this world marry and are given in marriage;
but those who are found worthy to attain that other world,
and resurrection from the dead, take neither wife nor husband; mortal no longer, they will be as the angels in heaven
are, children of God, now that the resurrection has given
them birth" (Luke 20. 34–6).

In the Kingdom of heaven where they are "mortal no
longer" and where there is no longer need for any institution of marriage to perpetuate the race, all will be sons of
God, for they will be born "not from human stock, not
from nature's will or man's but from God" (John 1. 13).
Voluntary celibacy is already the sign of this Kingdom,
and Jesus Christ who came to announce and to inaugurate
it, wished to give an example. Would it not occur to his
disciples, and especially his priests, that they should try to
give the same witness in their own lives? They were vowed
by a particular vocation to make ready for the eternal
marriage feast of which earthly marriage is only a reflec-

tion, representatives here below of him who is the Bridegroom of that spiritual marriage, and would they not be led to do as he did, and to abstain on earth from any other marriage, so as to consecrate themselves entirely to preparing for that wedding banquet of which the Eucharist is the Sacrament?

THE EXAMPLE AND TEACHING OF ST PAUL

Commenting on the seventh chapter of 1 Corinthians, Calvin concludes: "Now the upshot of all this disputation is that celibacy is better than marriage because it gives more liberty and enables men to serve God more easily, yet that it must not be imposed or of obligation in such a way that it would not be open to each man to marry when it seemed good to him."

Apart from the final clause, which rejects a definitive engagement to remain celibate, we must allow that Calvin has rightly discerned St Paul's teaching in this famous passage on marriage and virginity.

The Apostle declares at the outset that "a man does well to abstain from all commerce with women"; yet those who are bound in wedlock are not free to reject it: "he, not she, claims the right over her body, as she, not he, claims the right over his"; the liberty of each is thus limited by the will of the other. And this cannot be made a matter of reproach for the gift of continence is not given to everyone: "I wish you were all in the same state as myself; but each of us has his own endowment from God, one to live in this way, another in that. To the unmarried, and to the widows, I would say that they will do well to remain in the same state as myself, but if they have not the gift of continence, let them marry; better to marry than to feel the heat of passion" (1 Cor. 7. 7–9).

St Paul, after invoking his own example, returns to the

subject some verses later; he then invokes in favour of celibacy, a reason of a general nature: "This, then, I hold to be the best counsel in such times of stress, that this is the best condition for men to be in. . . . Not that thou dost commit sin if thou marriest; nor, if she marries, has the virgin committed sin. It is only that those who do so will meet with outward distress. But I leave you your freedom" (1 Cor. 7. 26–8).

Married people, the Apostle teaches, are engaged, by the very nature of their state, in a condition of disturbance imposed on them by conjugal life which can often be an obstacle or a difficulty for the seeking of God's Kingdom. This applies also to the use of all earthly goods: although in themselves they are helps, often necessary ones (and this can be the case with marriage), they can become obstacles in so far as one can become attached to them or enslaved to them or simply in so far as one has to devote time and energy to them in the ordinary course of things. Every Christian, therefore, must try to acquire an attitude of detachment in regard to these goods: whether rich or poor, he must be detached from riches; whether powerful or downtrodden, he must be free from the spirit of power; whether married or celibate, he must have a certain detachment about the joys of marriage which are only passing joys and the means of attaining to others which are final and lasting; that is what St Paul teaches in the following verses: "Only, brethren, I would say this; the time is drawing to an end; nothing remains, but for those who have wives to behave as though they had none; those who weep must forget their tears, and those who buy must renounce possession; and those who take advantage of what the world offers must not take full advantage of it; the fashion of this world is soon to pass away" (1 Cor. 7. 29–31).

If the goods of this world pass, it is therefore necessary not to fix one's heart on them, and it is even desirable to try to do without them; and for St Paul this is true of marriage also which, of its very nature, and by reason of the fresh duties which it creates, diminishes a man's freedom to consecrate himself entirely to preparing the way for the Kingdom:

And I would have you free from concern. He who is unmarried is concerned with God's claim, asking how he is to please God; whereas the married man is concerned with the world's claim, asking how he is to please his wife; and thus he is at issue with himself. So a woman who is free of wedlock, or a virgin, is concerned with the Lord's claim, intent on holiness, bodily and spiritual; whereas the married woman is concerned with the world's claim, asking how she is to please her husband. I am thinking of your own interest when I say this. It is not that I would hold you in a leash; I am thinking of what is suitable for you, and how you may best attend on the Lord without distraction. (1 Cor. 7. 32–5.)

It has been well said by Max Thurian, a brother of the Protestant Community of Thaizé, in his fine book on marriage and celibacy:

The apostle does not dramatize this division in the hearts of Christian husbands and wives. For them to love and seek to please one another is a way of serving the Lord indirectly. But it is an indirect service, whereas celibacy enables them to give all their time and all their preoccupations to the direct service of God and the Church. That is what Christ meant when he established the state of voluntary celibacy *for the Kingdom of God*. Thus voluntary celibacy, which brings about a resemblance to Christ which is not only spiritual but also physical and practical is a state particularly adapted to the service of the Kingdom. Like Jesus, the Christian celibate can be engaged without reserve, spiritually and humanly, in the ministry. He is a celibate not in order to live a more tranquil life, but to resemble Christ in his work for the Kingdom. All his energies and all his preoccupations must be directed to a living preaching of the

Gospel so as to hasten the return of Christ, if he is to be true to his calling.[1]

"So it is easy to understand", wrote Pius XII in his Encyclical on Virginity of March 25th, 1954, "why those who wish to consecrate themselves to God's service embrace the state of virginity as a liberation, so as to be more completely at the disposal of God and of their neighbour." Celibacy voluntarily undertaken makes one more available for the service of all; conjugal love involves of its very nature a certain exclusiveness which inevitably limits the scope of this universal charity, this availability without "accepting of persons".

It is true that St Paul's advice is addressed to all Christians and does not envisage directly those engaged in the work of the priesthood; but the motives which he here invokes cannot leave a bishop or a priest indifferent. The Protestant theologian A. Vinet grasped this clearly, when he wrote in his treatise on pastoral theology: "St Paul, who has claimed for all the right to marry, has nevertheless honoured celibacy, recommending it not merely as suitable in the dangerous times through which the Church was passing but as a means of giving oneself more completely to God. He was only reproducing the thought of Jesus Christ himself. St Paul, and his Master before him, in the passages just quoted, are not considering a particular class of person in the Church; but how should a counsel of perfection fail to apply, in the Church, to pastors especially?"

It seems, then, that St Paul's teaching can be applied to the priest in a quite special way; through celibacy he makes himself more available to all those whose servant he has become, without being bound by the ties of family and kinship; isn't it precisely a characteristic of the priesthood of the New Law that it is a priesthood according to the order of Melchisedech, that is to say, one freed from all

[1] Max Thurian, *Mariage et Célibat*, Paris, 1955, pp. 133–4.

dependence on carnal descent and from all distraction of family or race? Furthermore, the priest is charged by reason of his vocation with announcing the future Kingdom in which, beyond this passing world and beyond all transitory unions, the spiritual wedding between God and redeemed humanity is celebrated, of which marriage here on earth is only a reflection; it is fitting, then, that he should announce it not only by his teaching but also by his whole life.

This is certainly the perspective in which we must understand the prescription of 1 Timothy: "A bishop, then, must be one with whom no fault can be found, faithful to one wife" (1 Tim. 3. 2). How are we to understand this rule against a second marriage, unless the bishop's state requires of him in a special way, even in the sphere of marriage itself, a certain continence, a certain spirit of sacrifice?

THE USAGES OF THE EARLY CENTURIES

The Apostle's precept was not observed everywhere from the beginning: Tertullian, writing a treatise on monogamy about the year 217, expresses his indignation, in chapter 12, at seeing bigamists presiding over Churches, that is, bishops who had contracted two successive marriages. On the other hand, St Jerome, in a letter to Oceanus, finds it natural that this should be so provided that the first wife was dead before the future bishop was baptized. Many authors, too, see in St Paul's remark a counsel and not a real prohibition. It is not until the beginning of the fifth century, with Innocent I, that we find a definite decree forbidding clerics who have married twice to receive holy orders.

However, from very early times we can trace a tendency for members of the clergy to embrace celibacy, and the faithful came to consider those of them who lived in com-

plete continence as the most perfect: there is a great deal
of evidence for this, as Pius XI pointed out in his Encyclical on the Catholic Priesthood:

> At the end of the fourth century, to quote some outstanding
> examples, St Epiphanius bears witness that the law of celi-
> bacy already extended to subdeacons: "(The Church) does
> not admit to the diaconate, to the priesthood, to the episco-
> pate, to the subdiaconate, one who is still in the bonds of
> marriage and occupied with his children, even if he has been
> married only once; she accepts only a man who renounces
> family life or is a widower: and this is chiefly to be seen
> where the canons of the Church are carefully observed."
> But the most eloquent witness is the holy deacon of Edessa,
> Ephrem the Syrian, Doctor of the universal Church. . . . In
> one of his poems he addresses his friend bishop Abraham:
> "You are worthy of your name, Abraham, because you have
> become the father of many children. But because you have
> no wife, as Abraham had Sarah to wife, your wife is your
> flock. Bring up your sons in the truth; may they become for
> you sons of the Spirit and sons of the Promise that they
> may become heirs in Paradise. O blessed fruit of chastity
> in which the priest takes his delight."

It may be added that St Epiphanius also declares, in his
Treatise against the Heresies (Book 48), that the rule of
continence for the clergy goes back to the apostles themselves. Pope St Siricius goes further still in that he appeals
to the rule of the Old Testament to forbid priests all sexual
intercourse after their ordination; in a letter of February
10th, 385, to Himerius of Tarragona, we find the following:

> We have learnt that a large number of Christ's priests and
> deacons, long after their consecration, have continued to
> have children by their legitimate wives or even irregular
> sexual relations; they are said to justify themselves on the
> ground that in the Old Testament priests and ministers,
> according to the Scriptures, had the right to beget children.
> Well, then, will any defender of carnal pleasures reply to

these questions: Why has God given the following admonition to those who have charge of the sanctuary: "Keep yourselves apart, and be a holy people; remembering what God you worship" (Levit. 20. 7)? Why again must the priests live in the temple, far from their own houses, when the turn of their priestly class comes round once a year? It was that they might not have sexual intercourse, even with their wives. . . .

That is why the Lord Jesus also . . . declaring in the Gospel that he has come to fulfil the Law and not to destroy it, wished that the perfection of chastity should shine out in glory in the Church whose Spouse he is. . . . In virtue of these decisions we are all bound, priests and deacons, by an indissoluble law to submit our hearts and bodies to sobriety and chastity so that we may be altogether pleasing to God in the *daily* offering of sacrifice; for, says St Paul, "those who are in the flesh cannot please God" (Rom. 8. 8).

The letter ends by forbidding any priest or deacon to cohabit with his wife; it is only recalling previous legislation, supposedly well known, but it was to have considerable repercussions, for it was communicated by the pope himself to the bishops of Africa, and his arrangements were sanctioned some years later by Innocent I. So in the early years of the fifth century we find a good many local councils, in Spain, in Africa and in Gaul, prescribing that the Roman decision be put into effect and forbidding married priests and deacons to have relations with their wives.

In the east, during the same period, legislation is rather less severe, although the historian Socrates, in his *Ecclesiastical History*, reveals a very great diversity in practice: "In the east, all the leading priests, and the bishops, too, are not constrained by any law from exercising their marriage rights. . . . In Thessaly another custom has grown up: there, if a cleric has sexual intercourse with a woman whom he had married while still a layman, his functions are suspended." The Emperor Theodosius, in 420, allows bishops to keep their wives, but only if they observe continence; no law limits the marriage rights of priests. It is the Council of Trullo of 692 which finally fixes the practice of the Eastern Churches: the bishop is bound to absolute continence, and if he had been previously married he must despatch his wife to a distant monastery and support her; priests, deacons and subdeacons cannot marry after ordination, but if they had been previously married they retained their rights.

In the west, in spite of variations and countless local resistances, the requirement of chastity and continence for the priesthood becomes increasingly definite. Without spending time over historical details we must at least mention the important date in canonical legislation on the subject: in 1123 the Council of the Lateran declared that marriages contracted by priests, deacons or subdeacons after their ordination would be invalid, and further that candidates for sacred orders who were previously married must break off all relations with their wives; the Council of Trent, in its twenty-fourth Session, simply reinforces these decisions; finally the Code of Canon Law renews them and adds certain penalties for clerics who contravene them: Canon 987 adds that a married man cannot licitly receive any order without a special dispensation from the pope, and that if he had received major orders in ignorance without this dispensation he is forbidden to exercise them.

PROTESTANT OBJECTIONS

Attacks on celibacy have been frequent at all periods, and it would be impossible to mention them all. The Protestant reformation took up all those objections which had been made in the past, sometimes adding fresh touches to

them in accordance with the main principles of Protestant-
ism. Calvin, while admitting the superiority of celibacy
over marriage in actual practice, nevertheless in his commentary on 1 Timothy absolutely refuses to admit that anyone should oblige himself to it by a vow: "It must not be
imposed as of obligation in such a way that it would not
be open to each man to marry when it seemed good to
him. . . ." This same difficulty sometimes presents itself in
other forms: marriage being a holy institution of God, it
seems that no human power can forbid it to any category
of the faithful, and so not the clergy: "Consciences must
not be burdened", Calvin also writes, "by forbidding anyone to marry: each man must be left his freedom. It is
notorious that a great mistake was made . . . those who
have not shrunk from forbidding the clergy to marry have
been much braver than St Paul."

Now it does seem that St Paul himself expressly
approved a stable state of celibacy, one involving a definite
engagement which he considered it wrong to break; for in
1 Timothy (5. 9–15) he is speaking about the state of the
widows. He is advising his disciples about the conditions
which are to be fulfilled if women are to be put on the
"list of widows", so that some may not prove to have been
unwisely accepted, "incurring the guilt of breaking the
promise they have made". There had been, apparently,
some unfortunate incidents, and certain young widows had
been unfaithful to their promises, thus occasioning what is
really a piece of fresh legislation, tightening up the conditions of admission to this class. One cannot, then, invoke
St Paul's name against the principle of a stable institution
of celibacy in the Church or even an institution devoted
to an official service of the Church, for it seems clear that
the widows had certain official functions in the community,
and the earliest liturgical and canonical documents pre-
suppose an official institution: "When a widow is

appointed", Hippolytus of Rome prescribes, "she is to be installed only if she has lost her husband some time ago; if she has lost her husband recently, this charge is not to be entrusted to her: even if she is advanced in years she is to be tested for some time, for often the passions persist in those who give rein to them." So when the Church requires certain qualities, officially recognized, before admitting anyone to the community's service, she claims the power to require also a real engagement to the celibate life; what St Paul required of widows the Church has required more and more definitely of her clergy in the course of centuries, and she has done no more than to follow in the steps of the Apostle in her consciousness of her own apostolic power and of the requirements of a whole-hearted engagement to the service of the Christian community.

Can we say that according to St Paul's express statement celibacy cannot be accepted and willed except freely, and that the Church cannot therefore impose it as a necessary condition for receiving orders, since, moreover, a man is called by God to the priesthood? It is true that St Paul, writing to the Corinthians, denies that he has any wish to take away their liberty and repeats this several times. But it is all the more remarkable that in 1 Timothy he has required as one of the necessary qualities of a bishop that he should have been married only once; for this implies that he imposes perfect chastity on a bishop who is a widower. Is this not to declare equivalently that the gift of continence will be assuredly given to a man who is summoned by the Church to the episcopate and accepts this summons, submitting himself to the Apostle's requirements? When the episcopal body and, in particular, its visible Head have made these requirements more precise in the course of centuries, they have only borne witness to their consciousness of perpetuating the apostolic body and of having the same rights to determine the conditions of access to the priesthood in accordance with the circumstances and the opportunities of the time; to their consciousness also of being guided by the Holy Spirit and of imposing nothing which is beyond human possibilities, in the certitude that God will give the gift of continence to those who freely accept a vocation which is within the Church's competence; they may say what St Paul himself said at the end of his discourse on virginity in 1 Corinthians: "And I, too, claim to have the Spirit of God."

In fact the first Protestant reformers had quite a different complaint against ecclesiastical celibacy; they reproached it with being the cause of numberless scandals in the course of the centuries and with cloaking much loose conduct and irregularity. But on this ground of fact and the practical assessment of fact, without in any way failing to recognize and to admit very many weaknesses and failures, a Catholic must bow to the wisdom and prudence of the Church; and his personal experience, even if he has only the most casual acquaintance with a few priests, will show him that sacerdotal chastity is no empty phrase.

Fr Congar wrote recently:

> Contemporary Protestantism, freed to some extent from the burden of the sixteenth-century controversies, is beginning to have a better appreciation of the evangelical and biblical character of the state of continence or virginity. In 1743 John Wesley, the founder of Methodism, published his *Thoughts on Marriage and Celibacy*: always with an eye to the value of asceticism and with a realistic grasp of pastoral requirements, he recognized the ideal superiority of celibacy. . . . The Oxford Movement brought to Anglicanism some renewal of monastic life and there are nowadays clergymen who wish to remain celibate. Among Continental Protestants the notion of the religious life has attracted a certain amount of favourable attention (cf. in Germany the works of Fr Parpert). In France, the young

community of Taizé, sometimes called Cluny, observes celibacy and considers in a favourable light the vow of chastity.[2]

A member of the latter community, Max Thurian, recently published a book on the subject of marriage and celibacy while still feeling a certain objection to the imposition of celibacy on the clergy, he nevertheless shows its supreme fittingness for the ministry, and studies its inner and theological significance in the light of Christ's teaching and St Paul's; the last sentences of his fine book are of particular interest:

> By a clear understanding of this doctrine, and taking up a thoroughly human attitude, avoiding any artificial adaptation to the monastic past, the Christian celibate has a function to fulfil in regard to Christian husbands and wives, in the expression thus given by the Church to the love which the Creator has willed. The Christian celibate has renounced sexual life, but not as judging it impure. He knows its fulfilments and its requirements. He is a normal being. But in full awareness of what he is doing, without despising sexual life, without making virginity a superior ideal, but in order to be entirely at God's disposal, without restriction, in service and prayer, the Christian celibate has made the sacrifice of conjugal love in the interest of a greater love which extends to all men, the love of Christ which will fill all in all in life everlasting.

[2] Y. Congar, *Le célibat et les églises réformées*, in *Catholicisme*, Vol. 2, Col. 763.

CHAPTER VII

THE PRIESTHOOD OF THE

FAITHFUL

In 1520 Luther published a short work entitled *Babylonish Captivity of the Church*, which directly attacked Catholic teaching on the sacrament of Order and on the hierarchical priesthood in the Church:

> The true Church of Christ has no knowledge of this sacrament, and it has been invented by the pope's Church; not only is there no promise of grace in connection with it, but there is not even a mention of it in the whole of the New Testament. Now it is absurd to call something a divine sacrament when it cannot be shown even that it is divinely instituted. . . . All I can allow is that order is an ecclesiastical rite, like many others which have been introduced by churchmen of old, like the consecration of vessels, houses, vestments, water, salt . . . where nobody supposes that there is any sacrament. . . . In so far as Christians are priests at all, all of us Christians are priests. As for those whom we name as priests, they are ministers chosen by us, to do their service in our name, and the priesthood is nothing but the ministry.

Luther returned to the subject in his book *On the Abrogation of Private Masses*, and again declared that all Christians are priests by the same title:

Be certain, and let nobody persuade you to the contrary, if you wish to be a true Christian, that there is no visible and external priesthood in the New Testament save that which Satan has set up thanks to men's deceits. For us there is only one priesthood, that of Christ, through which he offered himself for us and offered us along with him. . . . This sacrifice is a spiritual one and common to all Christians. For we are all priests of the same priesthood, the priesthood of Christ, sons of Christ, the high priest. . . .

In this teaching of Luther's we may carefully distinguish two elements. There is first the negation of an external and hierarchical priesthood, and we cannot subscribe to this; for if it is true that Christ is the only high priest of the New Alliance, it is no less true, as the previous chapters have shown, that his priesthood has its sacrament here below, just as there is only one Body of Christ, at the Father's right hand, and that it is nevertheless contained in the sacrament of the Eucharist, it is Christ the high priest who acts and sanctifies in the bishops and priests of the Church.

Along with these negations Luther has also a positive teaching which is in accord with the Church's traditional doctrine: all Christians share in the priesthood of Jesus. This is a revealed truth which needs to be emphasized and which is also of importance for a better understanding of the sacrament of Order: for if laymen do not share in this sacrament, it is all the more necessary to determine how their participation in the priesthood of Jesus Christ is related to the special priesthood of the hierarchy.

THE INDICATIONS OF THE OLD TESTAMENT

The Old Testament recognizes a participation of the whole people in the priesthood, which in no way excludes the existence of a special category of priests. When the

Law was promulgated on Sinaï, God said to the people by the mouth of Moses: "Listen, then, to my voice, and keep your covenant with me; and I, to whom all the earth belongs, will single you out among its peoples to be my own. You shall serve me as a royal priesthood, as a consecrated nation" (Exod. 19. 5–6).

Isaias repeats this promise, now in the perspective of messianic times: "Strangers they shall be that tend your flocks for you, farm and vineyard alien hands shall till; for you, a higher name, a greater calling, priests and chosen ministers of the Lord your God" (Isaias 61. 5–6).

Unlike other peoples, who are engaged in profane labours, the people of God is to have a sacred ministry, an authentic sacerdotal mission in the world.

Alexandrian Judaism proves to have had particular interest in these texts and interprets them in a rather special way: there is a tendency to spiritualize the idea of priesthood more and more, to detach it more and more from the official worship of the Temple and to extend it to all the Jews of the dispensation and even to all pious souls outside Judaism.

Similar tendencies appear, within Palestine itself, in the Essene communities on which recent discoveries have shed quite a new light; in the community of Qumran, without depreciating the ritual sacrifices of blood in the Temple of Jerusalem, there was nevertheless a constant preoccupation with the spirit which ought to animate all acts of worship: a formalistic and quasi-mechanical performance of priestly actions and of worship in general could not suffice: true sacrifice is, first and foremost, interior sacrifice.

Indeed, to say nothing of the apocryphal writings in the last centuries before Christ, the sapiential books and the prophets had already opened up the way: reacting against a too material conception of sacrifice and of worship, the prophets and the psalms had proclaimed that true sacrifice consists in the virtuous acts of the faithful; the texts are familiar: "Wouldst thou have me eat bull's flesh, and drink the blood of goats? The sacrifice thou must offer to God is a sacrifice of praise, so wilt thou perform thy vows to the most High" (Ps. 49. 13–14). "Thou hast no mind for sacrifice, burnt offerings, if I brought them, thou wouldst refuse; here, O God, is my sacrifice, a broken spirit; a heart that is humbled and contrite thou, O God, wilt never disdain" (Ps. 50. 18–19). Such a spiritualization of the idea of sacrifice led necessarily to a corresponding spiritualization of the idea of priesthood, and to its extension to all those who offered to God, by virtuous living, a true and real worship.

A HOLY AND ROYAL PRIESTLY COMMUNITY

The teachings of the Exodus are taken up by St Peter and applied by him to Christians in a remarkable passage in his first Epistle, which is in all probability a baptismal catechism; the following exhortations are addressed to the newly baptized:

> You must put aside, then, every trace of ill-will and deceitfulness, your affectations, the grudges you bore, and all the slanderous talk; you are children new-born, and all your craving must be for the soul's pure milk, that will nurture you into salvation, once you have tasted, as you have surely tasted, the goodness of the Lord. Draw near to him; he is the living antitype of that stone which men rejected, which God has chosen and prized; you too must be built up on him, stones that live and breathe, into a spiritual fabric; you must be a holy priesthood, to offer up that spiritual sacrifice which God accepts through Jesus Christ. So you will find in scripture the words, Behold, I am setting down in Sion a corner-stone, chosen out and precious; those who believe in him will not be disappointed. Prized, then, by you, the believers, he is something other to

those who refuse belief; the stone which the builders rejected has become the chief stone at the corner, a stone to trip men's feet, a boulder they stumble against. They stumble over God's word, and refuse it belief; it is their destiny. Not so you; you are a chosen race, a royal priesthood, a consecrated nation, a people God means to have for himself; it is yours to proclaim the exploits of the God who has called you out of darkness into his marvellous light. Time was when you were not a people at all, now you are God's people; once you were unpitied, and now his pity is yours. (1 Peter 2. 1–10.)

Thus St Peter, drawing on the text of Exodus quoted above, but reading it in the Greek Septuagint translation, tells Christians twice over that they form a priestly community, or, to put it in full, that they constitute both the spiritual temple and the priestly community which offers in it a spiritual worship; in the Church, the spiritual temple of God, each of the faithful is a living stone, but the whole building rests upon a cornerstone which is none other than Christ himself. So it is through union with him that the baptized can offer this spiritual worship of prayer, charity and good works.

To this first aspect of the priesthood of Christians another must be added, described in the last part of the passage which we are considering, the Christian people, the royal priestly community, the consecrated nation, has been made the new people of God to proclaim the exploits of God. Here the priestly character of the Christian people has been put into relation not only with the spiritual sacrifice, but also with a real mission of evangelization, of preaching the message of salvation; there is a New Alliance, with a new people travelling to the true Promised Land, as is shown by the theme of the new Exodus prophesied by Isaias (Isaias 43. 16 *seq.*) which underlies all this passage; it is not, then, only the salvation of their own souls at which Christians must aim, as St Peter makes clear on several occasions in the same Epistle: "Your life among the Gentiles must be without reproach" (2. 12); they must "silence, by honest living, the ignorant chatter of fools; that is what God expects of you", and married women must have the desire to win over their husbands to the Word of God by their virtuous conduct (3. 1–2).

IN THE LETTERS OF SAINT PAUL

St Paul's teaching corresponds with St Peter's, and here too we can distinguish two titles in virtue of which all Christians participate in Christ's priesthood. A famous passage in the Epistle to the Romans describes the spiritual worship which we have to offer: "And now, brethren, I appeal to you by God's mercies to offer up your bodies as a living sacrifice, consecrated to God and worthy of his acceptance: this is the worship due from you as rational creatures." To give this passage its full force, it is not enough to say that Christians must offer themselves to God: the context shows that spiritual sacrifice is the fulfilment of God's will; and it is not simply a question of individual worship, as the following verses indicate: it is a worship which is performed within the Church, each member co-operating in his own way in the building up of the Body in its entirety (12. 3). The same Epistle, too, teaches us on several occasions that the apostolate, thus envisaged, is a privileged form of this spiritual worship: Paul gives God a spiritual worship by announcing the Gospel (1. 9): he is a priest of the Gospel of God "to make the Gentiles an offering worthy of acceptance, consecrated by the Holy Spirit" (15. 15–16).

In the Epistle to the Ephesians there are expressions which are closer to those of St Peter: Christians are integrated into a new organism of worship, a house of God,

God's residence, a holy temple, built on the corner-stone which is Christ (Ephes. 2. 18–22; cf. 1 Cor. 6. 19; 2 Cor. 6. 16).

In virtue of this, declares the Epistle to the Philippians (3. 3), the baptized form the true people of God, succeeding to the privileges of the Jewish people ("as for circumcision, it is we who practise it, we who serve God with the spirit"). The same Epistle also tells us that works of mercy are an integral part of this spiritual worship (4. 18), and preeminently of the apostolate (2. 17).

But it is again the Epistle to the Hebrews which offers the richest of instructions on the priesthood of Christians; they may be grouped in relation to two central themes.

The first theme is that of the approach of the people of God, travelling towards the true promised Land, to the true sanctuary into which Christ has first entered, bearing his sacrifice with him: whereas in the Old Law the high priest alone could penetrate beyond the veil, to the Holy of Holies, in the New Law the true high priest does not penetrate alone into the Holy of Holies of heaven, but brings us all in with him (cf. 9. 12; 10. 19 etc.); Christians may "come boldly before the throne of grace" (4. 16), and "through him [Christ] make their way to God" (7. 25), for the blood of Jesus "has opened up for us a new, a living approach, by way of the veil, I mean, his mortality" (10. 19–20). If at present Christians who are still in the world can approach the true sanctuary only by faith, that does make them penetrate it already in spirit, and they can offer to God "a continual sacrifice of praise, the tribute of lips that give thanks to his name" (13. 15): a spiritual sacrifice of praise, but also a sacrifice of good works: "meanwhile you must remember to do good to others and give alms: God takes pleasure in such sacrifices as this" (13. 16).

A second theme which constantly recurs in the Epistle

to the Hebrews is the *teleiosis* of Christians, their fulfilment in perfection: several passages declare that Christ
has been consummated in perfection as regards his priesthood by his sacrifice and his entrance into heaven; but
that also applies to the members of his Body: Christianity
must be perfect, having a genuine knowledge of the priesthood of Jesus (5. 10–14), having the "solid food" of the
"fullgrown" which comes after "our first lessons in Christ"
(6. 1); perfection was not realized by the levitical priesthood
but by Christ alone (7. 11), who, opening to us the way
of access to the true sanctuary, is able "where conscience
is concerned to bring the worshipper to his full growth"
(9. 8–9); by a single offering he has completed his work, for
all time, in those whom he sanctifies (10. 14), made them
fit to enter, with all the heralds of the faith, into possession
of the "promise fulfilled" (11. 39). In all these expressions
which speak of the perfection of Christians, it is impossible
not to think of a sort of priestly consecration: the word
teleiosis and its cognates are in fact technical expressions
used by the Septuagint translation to refer to priestly consecration; furthermore the main burden of the Epistle to
the Hebrews is precisely the superiority of Christian worship over that of the Old Law because it brings into a new
sphere of worship, in Christ's wake, all those who follow
him and whom his sacrifice has purified and made perfect.

So (and this is another point in which Christian worship is superior to levitical worship) "we have an altar of
our own, and it is not those who carry out the worship of
the tabernacle that are qualified to eat its sacrifice" (Heb.
13. 10); what altar is this? It does not seem to be the case
that the eucharistic table is directly intended, as some have
thought, but the body of Christ himself which is the altar
of his sacrifice. That is the Christian altar of which those
who carry out the worship of the temple of Jerusalem have
no right to eat, although it is a privilege of the priestly

caste to receive a share in the victims which have been immolated and offered. The whole movement of thought suggests that Christians have this right which is refused to those who carry out the worship of the tabernacle: for what would be the point of saying that the levitical priests are excluded, if nobody is allowed to participate? Christians, therefore, have an altar of which they have "a right to eat", which is a priestly privilege. If this altar is the heavenly altar of Christ's body, it seems nevertheless that there must be a form of worship which enables Christians to participate in this heavenly reality, a table at which it is possible to eat, and this table is the eucharistic table; the Christian faithful, by participating in the sacrifice of the Mass and in the Victim, have a true priestly function, which the Epistle to the Hebrews does not further describe but which is the subject of a fine commentary in the Encyclical *Mediator Dei et Hominum* of Pius XII.

PRIESTHOOD AND ROYALTY ACCORDING TO ST JOHN

The writings of St John contain many scattered remarks about the priesthood of all Christians.

In the second chapter of the Gospel, Jesus declares that the true sanctuary which will replace the temple of Jerusalem and which he will raise again in three days is his own body; he directs attention to the worship "in spirit and in truth", and the fourth chapter tells us that it will replace the figurative worship of the former economy. If Christians have "a bread which has come down from heaven", it will not be possible for them, nevertheless, to partake of it as they should, unless they "listen to the Father and learn" (6. 45); a purely material eating would be profitless without this spiritual eating: "only the spirit gives life, the flesh is of no avail" (6. 63); we must enter by faith into this world of heavenly realities where "all have the Lord for their teacher", but into which Christ alone can bring us, because he alone has seen the Father (6. 45–46).

This teaching, which comes directly from God to the hearts of all believers, is described by the first Epistle as an inward unction (1 John 2. 27–9): the outward teaching which is given to us by the hierarchy (cf. 1. 3–5; 2. 7 and 24) would be ineffective unless it were accompanied by an inward illumination which proceeds from this divine unction, a participation in the unction of him who is the Anointed One *par excellence*.

Since this unction of the Messias is a priestly one, and since we have a share in it, it is not surprising that the Apocalypse describes Christians as a "royal race of priests" (1. 6); each of them is destined to become a "pillar in the temple of God" (3. 12), that is, to play a personal part in the worship of the new temple which is the Church, the Kingdom of God which is both earthly and heavenly at the same time. So the twenty-four elders worship the Lamb, singing: "Thou wast slain in sacrifice; out of every tribe, every language, every people, every nation thou hast ransomed us with thy blood and given us to God. Thou hast made us a royal race of priests, to serve God; we shall reign as kings over the earth" (5. 9–10).

The faithful, whether already glorified or still living here below, thus form a realm of priests and reign over the earth; what does this mean save that the faithful, united to the glorified Christ, are leading the human race on the way to its fulfilment? All events have their value in relation to them, and their intervention acts with power upon the destinies of nations (6. 10); they struggle against Satan and his servants (12. 17) and must conquer under the leadership of the Lamb. The fourteenth chapter describes them, grouped around the Lamb, on Mount Sinaï which is the figure of the Church, and chapter 20 declares that they have been raised up by their baptism and reign with Christ for a thousand years; "over such the second death has no power, they will be priests of God, priests of Christ; all those thousand years they will reign with him" (20. 4–6): on the earth, during this period between the resurrection of Christ and the last coming, which is symbolized by the thousand years, the faithful raised up from the life of sin, share in the royalty and in the priesthood of the risen Lord; on the earth, they are already in some sort in heaven; their temple, which is none other than God himself and the Lamb, is above (21–2); and their good deeds help to weave the robe, the "linen of shining white", which is the wedding-garment of the Spouse of the Lamb (19. 8).

THE TWOFOLD CHARACTER OF THE CHRISTIAN'S PRIESTHOOD

From this brief examination of Scripture, the priesthood of Christians appears, first and foremost, as an extension of the priesthood of Jesus; he is the new temple, the new altar, the new sacrifice, the new priest. But all those who are members of his Body share the prerogatives of the Head; they are the living stones composing the new Temple which will not be finally completed until the Lord's *Parousia*; their whole life must be offered in sacrifice, united to the offering which Christ has made of his own, they can even now penetrate by faith, until such time as they do so in fact when they rise with their Head, into the true sanctuary where none may enter but the true high priest. Yet there is always one sacrifice, that of Christ, one priesthood, one temple of his body; for his life animates the whole organism of which he is the Head, and he inspires in us, by his Spirit, the faith and charity of the spiritual sacrifice, leading each of us to the Father.

On this showing the whole Christian life is a sacerdotal act, a sacrifice. Yet, without going beyond the indications of Scripture, it seems that we can find two complementary aspects of this priestly dignity of Christians; there is first the sphere of personal faith by which each Christian is guided in the various circumstances of his moral and religious life, everything which follows from our state as adoptive sons of God on the way to our heavenly homeland, but there is also the sphere of the special mission to which each is called within the Body of Christ which is the Church, gifts and charisms, vocations and states of life being diversified for the growth of the whole Body and the final achievement of the world's salvation. If the first aspect is predominant in the Epistle to the Hebrews, the second is frequently found in the Epistles of St Paul (Rom. 1. 9; 15. 15; Phil. 2. 17), and seems to underlie the vision of the Apocalypse, in which Christians, under the conduct of their Head, struggle against evil and vanquish it; the two aspects, finally, are brought together in the all-important text of the first Epistle of St Peter.

Now these two aspects are related to the two sacraments of Christian initiation, baptism and confirmation.

THE PRIESTHOOD OF THE FAITHFUL AND BAPTISM

Our participation in the priesthood of Jesus by baptism is one of the regular teachings of Christian tradition, and St Thomas, in his account of it, is only gathering the fruits of an old inheritance. The sacrament which gives us a share in the divine sonship of Jesus gives us also a share in his priestly anointing; this is not surprising when we remember that it is precisely the divine sonship communicated to the Saviour's humanity which constitutes Christ as Priest; by baptism we become Christians which means "anointed ones", as Theophilus of Antioch explained, before the end of the second century, in his *Book for Autolycus*. And very soon an anointing of oil is added to the essential rite of baptism to symbolize this inward effect.

By incorporating us with Christ, baptism unites us with his sacrifice, makes us die and rise again with him, as St Paul says: but each of us must still unite himself with this sacrifice by his free and personal act: "What has been celebrated in the sacrament", says St Leo the Great, "must nevertheless be realized as our deed." Each of us must personally "in this mortal frame . . . pay off the debt which the afflictions of Christ still leaves to be paid" (Col. 1. 24), "crucifying nature with all its passions, all its impulses" (Gal. 5. 24), in fine die freely to the life of sin, "mortify the leaven of yesterday which was all vice and mischief" (1 Cor. 5. 7–8), which St Paul calls, using a still more evocative term, the "old man".

Such is the spiritual sacrifice demanded of a Christian, which will enable him to unite himself to the life of the risen Lord by an increase of faith and charity in him; and it is still Christ who offers this sacrifice, it is he, as St Clement of Rome puts it, who is the "high priest of our offering", continuing to realize in time, through his grace, the salvation of men which he has won by his sacrifice. Each of our acts of virtue, inspired by faith and charity, by uniting us more closely with the risen Christ, unites us therefore more closely with his sacrifice and his priesthood.

The Fathers of the Church have added that this is also a participation in his royal priesthood, in conformity with the teaching of St Peter and of the Apocalypse, for Christ is King by his priesthood and in his sacrifice itself; for it is by this that he leads the Christian people to its true end, bringing back to the Father all those who follow him and granting to each the grace to follow him by offering himself in his turn: the Son of God who appears to St John at the beginning of the Apocalypse, wearing the long robe of the high priest, is the same who bears "written on his cloak, over his thigh, the King of kings and the Lord of lords" (Apoc. 1. 13 and 19. 16). In this dignity the Christian people shares, in virtue of the fact that each of the baptized can, freely and personally, unite himself to this sacrifice and so cooperate in this return of humanity to God. Through the sacrifice of Christ, and through the spiritual sacrifices of our whole lives, we regain the royalty which we lost through sin; that makes us slaves of the flesh, of the passions, of the devil, of all the forces of death; baptism, on the contrary, gives us back our empire over ourselves, over matter, which sin had lost for us. "Those are Kings", writes St Hilary commenting on Psalm 135, "in whom sin does not reign, those who are masters of their bodies, and who have an empire over the flesh which they have subdued and tamed. Thus they are Kings and God is also their King."

St Paul has expressed this bond between spiritual sacrifice and royalty in the following lines of the Epistle to the Romans (6. 12-3): "You must not, then, allow sin to tyrannize over your perishable bodies, to make you subject to its appetites. You must not make your bodily powers over to sin, to be the instruments of harm; make yourselves over to God, as men who have been dead and come to life again; make your bodily powers over to God, to be the instruments of right doing."

THE PRIESTHOOD OF THE FAITHFUL AND CONFIRMATION

Participating through his baptism in the royal priesthood of Jesus and in the divine anointing of his humanity, the Christian is nevertheless called to receive a new gift of the Spirit in confirmation, another sacerdotal anointing, which makes him fit to participate as an active member in the Church's apostolic activity and her struggle against the Kingdom of Satan; that, again, is the teaching of the Christian tradition which St Thomas has translated in his theology of sacramental "character".

This teaching has its roots in the New Testament; St Peter, in his discourse at the time when the Centurion Cornelius was converted (Acts 10. 38), compares the descent of the Holy Spirit upon Christ, after his baptism by John the Baptist, to anointing: "You have heard the story, a story which ran through the whole of Judaea, though it began in Galilee, after the baptism which John proclaimed; about Jesus of Nazareth, how God anointed him with the Holy Spirit and with power, so that he went about doing good, and curing all those who were under the devil's tyranny" (Acts 10. 37–8), that, moreover, was the teaching which Jesus had given in the synagogue of Nazareth, applying to himself the prophecy of Isaias about the anointing of the Servant of Yahweh (Luke 4. 14–21).

Now the effects of the descent of the Spirit upon Jesus already indicated by the texts which we have just cited, are so clearly similar to those which confirmation produces in us that the Fathers did not hesitate to relate the two mysteries to one another: so in confirmation is also seen an anointing by the Holy Spirit, by a power giving the newly baptized the grace to continue in his own person the public mission which Jesus began after his baptism by John the Baptist: the struggle against the devil, evangelization, the proclamation of God's Kingdom.

Thus it is not surprising that to the rite of the imposition of hands which remains the essential rite of confirmation and which signifies the descent of the Spirit, was very soon added another rite of anointing upon the head or forehead of the baptized: this is found as early as the *Apostolic Tradition* of Hippolytus of Rome: after baptism, the neophytes dressed and entered the Church where the bishop laid his hands on them, then he anointed them on the head with holy oil, saying, "I anoint you with holy oil in the Lord, the Father Almighty, Jesus Christ and the Holy Spirit."

This teaching is continued in the Latin Church, as is shown by the admirable prayers for the consecration of the Chrism on Maundy Thursday. In the preliminary prayer over the balsam which forms part of the chrism the bishop shows its priestly significance: "O God, you prepare the celestial mysteries and all their virtues; graciously hear our prayers and make ready for your mysteries this fragrant tear of the bark which is plentifully exuded by a flourishing bough and enriches us with priestly ointment. . . ." "May this balsam be for us . . . the everlasting chrism of a priestly anointing . . . so that all those who have been born anew in holy baptism and have been anointed with this liquid may receive an abundant benediction."

Then the splendid preface of consecration recalls that after the flood, an image of baptism, the dove carrying the olive branch, prefigured the anointing with olive oil: "This figure is realized when the waters of baptism have washed away our sins and the anointing with oil gives our countenances beauty and peace. So too you commanded your servant Moses, after washing his brother Aaron in water, to make him a priest by pouring this ointment upon him. But it received the supreme honour when you sent the Holy Spirit in the form of a dove upon your son Jesus Christ our Lord, after he had obtained baptism from John in the waters of Jordan." The prayer goes on to ask that the chrism may produce in Christians effects like those which were produced in Jesus: "May they receive the dignity of kings, priests and prophets, in accordance with the conditions laid down by you in this mystery."

Sharing in the priesthood of Jesus in a new way, the

newly-confirmed thus share in the sacerdotal mission of evangelization which Jesus publicly inaugurates after the descent of the Spirit; anointed with the perfumed oil, he can spread abroad "Christ's incense" (2 Cor. 2. 15), a comparison which St Thomas again makes, following Cyril of Jerusalem; he can "proclaim the exploits of God who has called (him) out of darkness into his marvellous light" (1 Peter 2. 9).

It cannot be doubted that this is a true sacerdotal grace; did not St Paul say that the proclamation of the Gospel of God made ready for God an acceptable offering? The Apostle is always in some sort a sacrificer who makes souls die to the world, so as to offer them to God, uniting them with the Lord's sacrifice.

This is also a participation in the Lord's royal power: "Those are Kings", said St Ambrose, commenting on Psalm 118, "who have received the grace to utter the word, to make the people bend their necks with a quasi-royal power, and to charm the souls of the saints. . . ." The newly-confirmed shares in the royal priesthood of Jesus in so far as he collaborates in the return to God of those who are redeemed by the sacrifice of their Head. So Pius XI wrote in the Encyclical *Ubi Arcano*: "Remind the faithful also that it is by working in the apostolate, privately and publicly, under your direction and that of your clergy, spreading the knowledge of Jesus Christ and making his love reign among men, that they deserve the splendid titles of a chosen race, a royal priesthood, a holy nation, a redeemed people."

THE PRIESTHOOD OF THE FAITHFUL AND THE CHURCH'S WORSHIP

Incorporated into the Church which is the Body of Christ, the faithful, we have said, all share in Christ's priesthood in the measure in which they are his members. Now this ecclesiastical Body has an official worship, in particular the Eucharist, which contains and sacramentally renews the one sacrifice of Jesus. The Mass, the sacrifice of the Church, is thus the very sacrifice of Christ but also the sacrifice of all Christians, who, by their baptism, can personally participate, unite their individual offering to that of their Head, whom the priest represents.

The Encyclical *Mediator* of Pius XII has insisted on this participation of the faithful in the offering of the Mass, and it distinguishes in it two aspects or principal grounds:

Now the faithful participate in the oblation, understood in this limited sense, after their own fashion and in a twofold manner, namely because they not only offer the sacrifice by the hands of the priest, but also, to a certain extent, in union with him. It is by reason of this participation, that the offering made by the people is also included in liturgical worship.

Now it is clear that the faithful offer the Sacrifice by the hands of the priest from the fact that the minister at the altar in offering a sacrifice in the name of all his members represents Christ, the Head of the mystical Body. Hence the whole Church can rightly be said to offer up the victim through Christ. But the conclusion that the people offer the sacrifice with the priest himself is not based on the fact that, being members of the Church no less than the priest himself, they perform a visible liturgical rite; for this is the privilege only of the minister who has been divinely appointed to this office: rather, it is based on the fact that the people unite their hearts in praise, impetration, expiation and thanksgiving with the prayers or intention of the priest, even of the High Priest himself, so in the one and same offering of the victim and according to a visible sacerdotal rite, they may be presented to God the Father. It is obviously necessary that the external sacrificial rite should, of its very nature, signify the internal worship of the heart. Now the sacrifice of the New Law signifies that supreme worship by which the principal offerer himself, who is Christ, and in union with him and through him all the members of the mystical Body, pay God the honour and reverence that are due to him. . . .

In order that the oblation by which the faithful offer the divine victim in this sacrifice to the heavenly Father may have its full effect, it is necessary that the people add something else, namely the offering of themselves as a victim.

This offering in fact is not confined merely to the liturgical sacrifice. For the Prince of the Apostles wishes us, as living stones built upon Christ the corner stone, to be able as "a holy priesthood, to offer up spiritual sacrifices, acceptable to God by Jesus Christ. . . ."

This uniting of the faithful with the offering of the Eucharist is made clear by the rites themselves: they bring the priest the materials for the sacrifice, the bread and the wine, or at least the alms by which they share in the material expenses of the Church's worship and good works; the liturgical prayers often refer to their presence and their part in the offertory; they are publicly united with the priest's prayer, or, at least, the Mass-server represents them in this function; finally and above all, they share in the victim by communion in the Body and Blood of the Saviour.

THE PRIESTHOOD OF THE FAITHFUL AND THE HIERARCHICAL PRIESTHOOD

Although members of a society for worship, the faithful are not all members by the same title, and the priesthood which is common to all the baptized and confirmed is not of the same order as that of the hierarchy. Combating the errors of Luther, which we have mentioned above, and similar errors which have shown signs of reappearing in the recent past, the Encyclical *Mediator* has again vigor-

ously insisted on the distinction between the two priest-
hoods.

The distinction is easily grasped if we remember what
the Church means by a sacrament, a sensible sign which
contains a visible reality and which makes it present and
operative in the Church; since the latter continues here
below the sacerdotal function of her Head, it is fitting that
his priesthood should be represented in her; each member
of the Body of Christ, participating only as a particular
member—the priesthood of the entire Body, cannot represent the Head, the Leader of the sacerdotal Body in his
permanent and inalienable function. The sacrament of
order has as its effect, as the preceding pages have shown,
precisely to constitute certain chosen men as representatives
of the Priesthood of the Head of the Mystical Body; as
such, they are no longer merely members of the sacerdotal
Body, they are the Head himself represented by them and
acting through them upon the other members. It has been
already pointed out that this traditional teaching is rooted
in the teaching of Scripture itself and has been copiously
illustrated by the Fathers of the Church.

To gain a coherent idea of the relations between the
hierarchical priesthood and that common to all the faithful,
it is therefore necessary to recall that the former is not
only conferred by a special sacrament, but also that, in
its expression and in its power, it is a *sacramental* priesthood; with all the necessary precautions, one can say that
there is the same difference between these two participa-
tions in Christ's unique priesthood as between the eucharistic Body of Christ and the mystical Body of which all
Christians are members: bishops and priests in their special
priesthood, are not simply members of the mystical Body,
they are the sacrament of the priesthood of the Head.
Personally they are also members of this Body, and their
personal sanctity does not depend upon their advancement

in the ranks of the hierarchy. But, since the Word has been made visible in a Body of flesh, it is a constant law of our condition as Christians upon earth that we must participate in invisible realities by means of sensible and visible signs, conveying heavenly grace; it is as such that bishops and priests are, each in their proper place, sacraments of the priesthood of Jesus who, by them, continues to teach, to sanctify and to pardon. The unity of the individual members with their invisible Head is brought about through them, through unity with the Church's visible priesthood.

This teaching receives astonishing expression in the letter of Ignatius of Antioch: "Subject yourselves to the bishop," he writes to the Magnesians (13. 2), "as Christ according to the flesh was subject to the Father and the apostles to Christ, and to the Father and the Spirit so that his union may be at the same time fleshly and spiritual." To unite oneself spiritually to Christ the high priest, glorified at God's right hand, is not sufficient: we must also go to him by way of the visible priesthood of those whom he has chosen and appointed to represent him.

Christian laymen, then, are not in any way humiliated or lessened in their dignity as sons of God in the presence of the hierarchical priesthood, for they are not obeying men, confessing their faults to men, asking for the eucharistic bread from men; in each case it is with Christ himself that they have to do. That great Christian Manzoni had a clear understanding of this and Pius XI in his Encyclical on the priesthood quotes these admirable words of his:

When a priest, groaning within himself at the thought of his unworthiness and the sublimity of his functions, has put his consecrated hands on our heads, when, humiliated to find himself the dispenser of the Blood of the Alliance, amazed on each occasion to utter the words which give life when, a sinner himself, he has absolved a sinner, we ourselves, rising from before his feet, realize that we have suffered no indignity. . . . We have been at the feet of a man who represented Jesus Christ . . . we have been there to gain the characteristics of free men and of God's children.

We can go a step further: since it is from the heart of the Christian people itself that the Church summons those who are to become her priests, we must recognize here also an aspect and a privilege of the priesthood which is common to all the faithful. "Let them be persuaded", said Pius XI again, "that to help with the recruitment of the secular and regular clergy is the best way in which they can participate in this dignity of the royal priesthood which the Prince of the Apostles attributes to all the people of the redeemed."

SELECT BIBLIOGRAPHY

BLIGH, John, S.J.: *Ordination to the Priesthood*, London and New York, Sheed and Ward, 1956.

JURGENS, W. A.: *The Priesthood, a translation of the* Peri Hierosynes *of St John Chrysostom,* New York, Macmillan, 1955.

DUCHESNE, LOUIS: *Christian Worship: Its Origin and Evolution*, London, S.P.C.K., and New York, Macmillan, 1903.

CONGAR, Yves M. J., O.P.: *Lay People in the Church*, London, Bloomsbury Publishing Co., and Westminster, Md, Newman Press, 1957.

VAN ZELLER, Dom Hubert: *The Gospel Priesthood*, London, Burns Oates, and New York, Sheed and Ward, 1956.

LEBRETON, Jules, S.J., and ZEILLER, Jacques: *The History of the Primitive Church*, London, Burns Oates, and New York, Macmillan, four volumes, 1942–8.

SCHAMONI, Wilhelm: *Married Men as ordained Deacons*, London, Burns Oates, and Springfield, Illinois, Templegate, 1955.

The Twentieth Century Encyclopedia
of Catholicism

*The number of each volume indicates its place in
the over-all series and not the order of appearance.*

TWENTIETH CENTURY ENCYCLOPEDIA OF CATHOLICISM

All titles are subject to change.